DEC

P9-DMS-211

MURDER IN THE NEWS

MURDER
IN THE **NEWS**
AN **INSIDE LOOK** AT HOW
TELEVISION COVERS CRIME

ROBERT H. JORDAN JR.

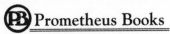
Prometheus Books

59 John Glenn Drive
Amherst, New York 14228

Published 2017 by Prometheus Books

Cover image © Media Bakery
Cover design by Liz Mills
Cover design © Prometheus Books

Inquiries should be addressed to
Prometheus Books
59 John Glenn Drive
Amherst, New York 14228
VOICE: 716–691–0133 • FAX: 716–691–0137
WWW.PROMETHEUSBOOKS.COM

21 20 19 18 17   5 4 3 2 1

Library of Congress Cataloging-in-Publication Data

Names: Jordan, Robert H., Jr., 1943- author.
Title: Murder in the news : an inside look at how television covers crime /
    by Robert H. Jordan, Jr.
Description: Amherst : Prometheus Books, 2017. | Includes index.
Identifiers: LCCN 2017025260 (print) | LCCN 2017041482 (ebook) |
    ISBN 9781633883284 (ebook) | ISBN 9781633883277 (hardback)
Subjects: LCSH: Crime and the press—United States. | Crime on television. |
    Crime—Press coverage—United States. | Television broadcasting—Social
    aspects—United States. | Television broadcasting of news—United States. |
    BISAC: LANGUAGE ARTS & DISCIPLINES / Journalism.
Classification: LCC PN4888.C8 (ebook) | LCC PN4888.C8 J67 2017 (print) |
    DDC 070.4/49364152—dc23
LC record available at https://lccn.loc.gov/2017025260

Printed in the United States of America

For, Sharon, Karen, Christian, Vivian, and Jay with everlasting love.

CONTENTS

Preface   9

Acknowledgments   15

Introduction   19

Chapter One: Second-Rate Murders . . . Really?   25

Chapter Two: Murder Coverage as a Reflection of Society   53

Chapter Three: The History of the Changing
              Broadcast Format   79

Chapter Four: Survey—Deciding Which
              Murder Stories to Cover   107

Chapter Five: Good Guys vs. Bad Guys   127

Chapter Six: Bad Guys vs. Bad Guys   141

Chapter Seven: The Phantom Audience in Us All   157

Chapter Eight: Perspective and Truth   175

Chapter Nine: Realigning the Process for Covering Murders   189

Notes   211

Index   231

PREFACE

In the summer of 1994, I was frantically rushed out the door of my Chicago television station to cover a story about the indictment of a popular local African American congressman, Mel Reynolds. Arriving at his South Side office—in a 75 percent black district—I was met by an enormous swarm of my media colleagues: reporters, camera crews, television field producers, radio reporters, newspaper reporters, all from various media operations—a throng of impatient and eager journalists, sensing that this was the "big" story of the day.

We were waiting to ambush Reynolds when he entered or left his office, prepared to shout questions at him about the salacious charges of sex with an underage campaign worker.[1] We didn't know if he was inside or not, but we were prepared to stay as long as it took to get a picture of him and hopefully a sound bite.

A Cook County grand jury had just indicted Reynolds on charges of criminal sexual assault, child pornography, and obstruction of justice. Reynolds had vehemently denied having the affair, which allegedly took place two years before, in 1992. His accuser was a woman who alleged that she was sixteen years old when the relationship occurred. This was the kind of sensational story that works reporters up into a frenzy, each station trying to outdo the other, searching for mindless, inane bits of information that the station can call "exclusive material."

Why was the indictment of Mel Reynolds so important? Why was this story leading off the newscast of each national evening news program? Why was this front-page, "top-of-the-fold" news?

The allegations were "hot" because they contained all the ele-

9

ments that often drive a story to become sensational—or in the eyes of the television editor or producer—worthy of leading off the show. This was a "huge" story, and any producer would want to "open" the newscast with blaring headlines and BOLD graphics.

But, before I dissect this story and examine the features that set the Reynolds report apart from the everyday sex case, let me tell you why I have not forgotten that day and why being in that neighborhood had such an impact on my life—eventually prompting me to write this book.

While standing there waiting for Reynolds to show up, I felt a tap on my shoulder. Standing behind me was a black woman who appeared to be around sixty years old. She smiled and said, "Hello, Mr. Jordan." (By then, I had been reporting and anchoring the news in Chicago for more than twenty years, so I was well known to many residents.) I shook her hand and said hello. Again smiling, she said, "I am so happy that all of you reporters are here to cover that awful story about the three boys who were shot yesterday."

I had no idea what she was talking about and told her so. Stepping back, frowning, and appearing tense, she said, "If you are not here for the shooting of those boys, then why are you here?" I told her that I hadn't heard about the shooting and was there to cover the indictment of Congressman Reynolds.

Her mouth fell open in disbelief as her eyes began to squint. Poking me in the chest with her index finger, she stepped up closer and, with words spurting out in a forceful staccato, said, "Well, now you know about the shooting. What are you going to do?" I stammered and tried to find an adequate answer but was cut off in midsentence. "To hell with Mel Reynolds," she said. "Who cares that he slept with that strumpet? Yeah, it was bad, but a human life—three human lives . . . The shooting of three of our young boys is so much more an important story."

She paused, then said, "I'm ashamed of you."

After glaring at me for a couple of seconds with scorching eyes, she turned and stormed off. I was frozen—mentally searching for something sufficient to say—but just stood there with my mouth open and a stupid expression on my face.

All my fellow reporters had witnessed my public humiliation. One walked over and said, "She's right, you know, we *should* all be covering that shooting instead of Mel." I already knew that, too. But it was her stinging criticism—the biting, truthful words from a woman whose name I will never know—that dug deeply into my soul: "I'm ashamed of you." The words echoed, nonstop, in my mind for weeks.

But, innately, I knew why we were there. The story of the rise and fall of Mel Reynolds had all the "juicy" elements media outlets crave; he was born to poor parents in Mound Bayou, Mississippi, in 1952, and his family moved north, where he excelled in school. Reynolds became a Rhodes Scholar, earning an LLB from Oxford University in 1979. He also completed a master's degree in public administration at Harvard's Kennedy School of Government in 1986.[2]

Reynolds said to me years later that his poor, uneducated grandmother had told him something, when he was a child, that stuck with him for the rest of his life. "Mel," she said, "the longer you stay in school, the less you will have to tote."[3] That simple, straightforward axiom was something he never forgot.

After graduation, instead of taking a high-profile, big-money job, Reynolds returned to his disadvantaged Chicago neighborhood to work. He started an organization—American Scholars Against World Hunger—to fight famine in Africa. He developed a reputation as a determined community activist, participating in an antidrug campaign on Chicago's South Side. He also worked to provide scholarships for needy students. He had two unsuccessful campaigns for Congress before finally winning a seat to the Second Congressional District.

But titillating rumors had already begun to surface, hinting at a darker side that might shatter his made-for-Hollywood image, a Mr. Hyde creeping in the shadows who could destroy his golden boy reputation. Add the whispers of forbidden sex into the equation and it became apparent why we were all there (even though these hints were unproven allegations).

There was no way I could explain all that to the neighborhood woman. I couldn't just reassign myself to another story without going through the editorial hierarchy back at the station. And any excuse I could have provided to her would have just sounded hollow—because ethically she was right. (The homicides of three teens must certainly be more important than a consensual sex crime by a public official—ask the families of the deceased, and there would be no argument.)

The stern scolding by the passionate neighborhood woman was something I couldn't forget.

Going forward, I struggled with the issue of why some murder stories gained "sensational" status while other killings, like those of the three boys, were virtually ignored. The puzzle drove me to enter a doctoral program at Loyola University in Chicago to examine how the audience impacts the decisions news producers make.

That was sixteen years ago. Since then, I have gained even more knowledge about this subject because of my research when writing my dissertation. I consider this project to be a postdoctoral investigation, as I have interviewed twenty additional individuals who are key gatekeepers in news organizations, to gain a supplementary understanding of this complex topic.

I also bring forty years of journalistic understanding to this project, including experiences gathered from hundreds of obscure and high-profile murder stories over the last four decades. Some of these stories are unique because they represent groundbreaking reports or stories that were revolutionary in changing perceptions.

I hope that students in journalism schools across the country will consider much of the information in this book as they go about their jobs reporting the news. The questions raised here need to spark an inextinguishable curiosity—about news coverage of murders—that is debated over and over so that journalists can try to remain thoughtful and objective when considering which stories to trumpet and which stories to push to the back pages.

And to the layperson or non-journalist: As observers, viewers, and readers of news material, after digesting this book you will find it difficult to be "spoon-fed" news reports, ever again, without examining them critically. Armed with this knowledge, you will immediately recognize and understand why some news stories are heavily weighted, on one hand, while others—similar in nature—are passed over, or merely given a smidgen of attention.

Finally, every newsperson needs to experience a tap-on-the-back moment when someone or some experience shocks him or her to the core, sparking a flash of enlightenment and clarity. That stinging epiphany should remind every reporter, producer, and editor about the true and ethical mission of our work as journalists; otherwise we can fall victim to wrongly conceived notions about what is *really* important.

ACKNOWLEDGMENTS

As a recently retired television news journalist, I wanted to share many of the lessons learned over a nearly fifty-year career. But to do so has required the assistance of many people who have helped shape my life, worldview, and understanding of ethical principles and journalistic values.

My first blessing was to be born of parents who set very high standards of excellence—and demonstrated the value of dogged determination. My father, Dr. Robert Jordan, was a former college science and biology teacher who went back to school in midlife to become a dentist, and my mother, Millicent Dobbs Jordan, was a professor at Spelman College in Atlanta for four decades. Their urging to shun mediocrity was a constant drumbeat that my younger twin brothers, Dobbs and James Jordan, and I were taught.

At WGN-TV, where I spent the vast majority of my career, I worked with many fine journalists, some of whom you will meet in this book. Two special colleagues deserve recognition: cameraman, Richard "Ike" Isaac and my coanchor, Jackie Bange. Ike and I were partners who worked as a team for several decades covering thousands of stories. He became not only one of my best friends but a colleague, confidant, and brother. On a breaking story when chaos was all around and you absolutely had to have the video, Ike was the cameraman who would always come back with the shots.

Jackie Bange was my coanchor and dear friend for almost twenty-two years. At one point we were the longest-running anchor team in Chicago. I called her my TV wife. We covered so many breaking news stories that we began to think alike. We learned to lean on each other for support and knowledge; Jackie was always cool and calm and never agitated. We developed a tool for remaining loose and unflustered (after a first segment filled with murders, disasters, and other calamities) that consisted of dozens of handshake moves. A video of the routine went viral on YouTube and had been viewed at last count 7,244,619 times and counting, in June 2017. The site is called, "What News Anchors Do during Commercial Breaks."

For thirty-five years I have had the same television agent, Paul Julian. Paul has remained a dear friend and confidant whose knowledge and savvy have been valuable attributes in guiding and advising me through several general managers and many news directors. Paul is the best!

I offer my deepest thanks to my literary agent, Hilary Claggett, who is with the Rudy Agency. Hilary read the manuscript and believed in the project from the beginning. She was able to be in contact with several publishing companies and was able to close the deal with Prometheus Books. Initial proofreading and editing began with Tricia Parker from Tricia Parker Communications. Tricia introduced me to Hilary and has been a huge supporter of my book from the beginning.

At Prometheus Books, I want to acknowledge the many talented people who helped to shape the manuscript into a tighter, more concise book. Steven L. Mitchell, editor in chief at Prometheus Books, led the fabulous team. Because of Steven's wise counsel I was able to focus more clearly on the important content of the book. Hanna Etu began the editing process by issuing strict deadlines for revising the bibliography and securing releases from interviewees. I can't say enough good things about my copyeditor at Prometheus Books, Jeffrey Curry. I am extraordinarily fortunate to have had Jeffrey's insightful guidance throughout to sculpt and remove the literary fat so that the lean could be seen more clearly. Jeffrey's broad vision to understand whole chapters of the manuscript brought my wanderings under control to sharpen the focus of the book.

Finally, this book would not have been possible without the loving assistance of my devoted wife, Sharon. I learned nearly fifty years ago to not let any writings of mine leave my hands without first getting her approval. A librarian by training—working at the American Library Association for twelve years—Sharon's strong literary training has been a wonderful asset that I have been lucky to have so near. Our only child, Karen Farr, a Spelman College graduate, who sought her graduate school training at Medill School Journalism, has followed us both into a career of writing. Karen is a weekend anchor/reporter at ABC station WLS-TV Channel 7 in Chicago. Her husband is also a journalist, Christian Farr. Chris is a reporter/weekend morning anchor at NBC station WBBM-TV Channel 5 in Chicago. The encouragement I received from all of them has been extraordinarily inspiring as I have sought to create a clear path for them to follow.

I grew up in a family that cherished books. My grandfather, John Wesley Dobbs—born just seventeen years after slavery—had a library in his house. My mother had a library in her home, and I have one in mine. I hope this book becomes a meaningful part of your collection.

INTRODUCTION

For months leading up to the election of Donald Trump as the forty-fifth president of the United States, news coverage of the bitter campaign included references to crime in general and murder rates across the country, in particular. Chicago was often emphasized by President Trump as an example of a city where shootings were out of control. Trump and his opponent, Hillary Clinton, used social media, particularly Twitter, to fawn for votes while lambasting the press (Trump more so than Clinton), and journalists were often ridiculed by Trump when he disliked coverage he received.

But, news coverage is sifted and strained before it is disseminated. Most people have no idea that the information that is provided to us from television, radio, and newspaper reporters has been filtered through a sieve of newsroom gatekeepers who decide what's news and what isn't. This has always been the case. But today, that *process* of deciding, as an example, which murder stories to cover and which to ignore, has become an accepted practice.

As a television news reporter in Chicago since 1973, I have observed the process change, almost beyond recognition. Sadly, serious journalism in many newsrooms has morphed into "infotainment"—a disgraceful portmanteau that illustrates the inexorable decline of standards that are inherent in the press and that buttress the protections established in the First Amendment to the Constitution.

When I began working in television in 1970, the practice of using official "sources" was the established way to authenticate information to be "truthful" and was an accepted manner of verifying information. For decades, assignment editors, producers, and city desk editors allowed establishment "hacks"—the PR spokesperson, or the PIO (public information officer) from police departments across the country—to give self-aggrandizing explanations of events that, most of the time, the newsroom gatekeepers accepted as fact.

So, up until five or ten years ago, when battered and abused people complained to reporters that they had been beaten, kicked, and knocked around by arresting police officers, most of the time reporters ignored the complaints, feeling that the subjects were just disgruntled revenge seekers who were angry that they had been arrested in the first place.

Now, we can pinpoint to the day, the time in American history, when newsroom personnel across the country were shocked into reality. It was the moment, a quarter of a century ago, when video was broadcast of LA police officers, using nightsticks, beating motorist Rodney King on March 3, 1991. Since then, police misconduct has resulted in several officers being prosecuted while the public has watched, over and over again, as dashboard cameras and body cam videos have exposed the questionable brutality of certain police officers during stressful encounters.

The Rodney King video was stunning to watch. First of all, no one in our newsroom could believe that police officers could take part in such a violent action. King was on the ground most of the time while officers pummeled and kicked him into submission—it was shocking. I remember that we initially thought it must have been a scene from a movie being shot in LA. We refused to believe that the video we were watching with our own eyes could be true.

Yet, by 2015 and 2016, protest marches had become commonplace in the streets of many major American cities. A new movement, with the chant "Black Lives Matter," has drawn marchers to the doorsteps of police departments, and leaders have demanded that change take place and officers desist from exercising deadly force so quickly. Counter marchers from "Blue Lives Matter" (a group supporting police) have clashed with Black Lives Matter, and near riots have resulted.

All this might not have happened so swiftly and with such explosive and revolutionary force if there hadn't been video of the incidents. The public could, for the first time, see in unbelievable clarity that atrocities could and do take place—and in all likelihood had been occurring all along. Reporters and editors had, for decades, elected to believe the establishment version of events as if they were gospel. Now, these same filterers were faced with an uncomfortable reality that journalists could no longer just take the word of administrative mouthpieces without also considering the other side of the story, too.

When I decided to write this book, I realized that it would be easier for the public to digest if I narrowed my discussion of journalist decision making to just one element of reporting: news coverage of murders. In some respects, the treatment of murder is the perfect way to analyze how newsrooms work in getting information out to the public. And while the method of information dispersal has changed over the years—Facebook, Twitter, cell phone video, and other social media apps all come to mind—one fact remains unchanged: murders are detestable, abhorrent crimes that many times draw police and their critics together in search for the perpetrator. Later on in the book I will discuss police misconduct and its effect on murder coverage in more detail.

When you ask judges, mayors, chiefs of police, and ordinary citizens about combatting crime in Chicago—specifically shootings and gun deaths—the first reaction is a blank stare followed by a side-to-side head shake. After a moment or two you hear, "I don't know what the hell is going on—it's just crazy."

The out of control gun violence in Chicago has erupted today because of policies put in place decades ago. The gun-happy teens who are shooting each other in cold-blooded, pitiless fashion have been trained and encouraged by repeat offender gang leaders. The invisible leaders—the generals who run the gangs—have spent nearly all their lives in the "gray bar university penitentiaries" that have been their training grounds for learning how to commit crimes more skillfully each time they recidivate and later return to the streets.

On the other side of the equation are the men and women in blue who are sworn to uphold the law and bring the shooters to justice—getting them off the streets so law-abiding citizens can live in peace. The clear majority of these officers are good, sensitive, caring men and women who place their lives on the line each day to maintain the peace. And therein lies the problem. The conflict between both sides has reached the boiling point, and tensions in many inner-city neighborhoods are frayed and can break loose at any time, resulting in rioting and disorder.

Monitoring this uneasy dance between police and the communities they are sworn to protect is the press. Journalists assume the responsibility of carefully watching communities as social forces exert extreme pressures on some areas: crime, unemployment, rival violent street gangs, and other negative factors that undermine the abilities of residents to live congenial lifestyles.

But—and here is the tragedy—in many major American cities, the public rarely gets a true picture of these neighborhoods and the people who struggle, by the hour, just to survive and eke out an existence. Media outlets rarely spend the necessary amount of time in these sorrowful neighborhoods telling the gritty tales of survival that go on in millions of homes around the country. These stories are ignored and forgotten.

Likewise, the stories of successful minority families who, by the untold thousands, have become happy middle- and upper-class citizens rarely have their stories told. We seldom hear the inspiring tales of African American Big Ten or Ivy League graduates who have become titans of business and industry. Instead, the exploits of a small 2 percent—the destructive "gangbangers"—dominate the headlines and lead off each newscast.

This book will take you behind the scenes as news workers—who in the vast majority of cases are hardworking, diligent journalists— make everyday, split-second decisions about the murder coverage you'll receive and the incidents you'll never hear about.

Yet even though journalists work hard to give accurate reports during news coverage, at a morning rally in Atkinson, New Hampshire, Donald Trump, during his presidential campaign, criticized media outlets, as he often did. "They're scum," Trump said. "They're horrible people. They are so illegitimate. They are just terrible people."[1] While Trump is not referencing crime coverage, per se, he did often complain about big-city crime. His disparaging remarks about the press can affect the way murders are covered. Ironically, Trump forgets that he is a byproduct of the media himself.

Some argue that it is not journalists' responsibility to drive social change. Instead, according to this viewpoint, reporters are merely conduits through which information flows out to the masses. But I feel that approach is a "cop-out" since, in reality, the stories journalists report do have an impact and can influence public policy and affect the way we think and perceive others to be. Reporters understand this and often work to craft their stories to avoid showing partiality.

Journalists know the dangers of muzzling the press, and countless reporters have lost their lives while trying to inform the public about matters that authoritarian governments wish to squelch. So, it is with that philosophy in mind that I approached this book—to hopefully stimulate discussion about how media outlets cover murder in the news.

Chapter One

SECOND-RATE
MURDERS . . . REALLY?

Lasciate ogne speranza, voi ch'intrate.

Abandon all hope, ye who enter here.
—Dante Alighieri, *The Divine Comedy*

There are scruffy neighborhoods on the West and South Sides of
Chicago, within clear view of opulent downtown office buildings, where some homes are pockmarked from stray bullets and
bloodstained sidewalks indicate a trail of misery and sadness. You
don't have to be brave to wander around in these ghettos, just ill-
advised. Dante's frightening warning to the lost souls entering hell
could easily apply to outsiders venturing into some wasteland blocks
in Chicago.

Eighty-five zip codes comprise Chicago; six of them are where
street gangs, fighting for control of drug turf, routinely try to kill each
other. In these slaughter zones, shootings are so familiar that television journalists often make decisions to ignore a murder because it
is routine, or what police call "gang related" and repetitive: nothing
new.

The ratta-tat-tat of automatic weapons fire can be heard echoing
through the decaying three-flat buildings with such regularity that
the sounds are no longer startling. Like a broken car alarm—that
goes off so often no one runs to the window to check—the gunfire

has stopped making residents skittish or fall to the floor; it has become routine.

The appalling regularity of shootings, especially on weekends, forces law-abiding citizens to seek shelter in their homes or risk becoming new faces on the coroner's tally board of innocent victims.

Murder has been around as long as humans have been upright. But some murders, or the circumstances surrounding them, fascinate us more than other homicides. What is it about these "special cases" that cause them to become sensationalized in the news while other homicides receive little or no attention? When we view an astonishing murder story on television or read about the death in a newspaper, we rarely question what it is about this particular killing that caused it to become so important. We just assume that the murder of this victim merited being given front-page, top-story attention. Indeed, the murder of every human being should be considered so significant that news coverage is given—in an equal manner—to these events. But that is not the case.

When television assignment editors and producers learn of a murder, they immediately make an instinctive decision—based on who the victim was and the circumstances of the death—that will determine how the story will be covered.

Something interesting about a particular incident begins to appeal to an intuitive judgment that journalists have about certain stories (some call it a nose for news). That innate feeling becomes "the hook" on which various "elements" are hung, allowing the story to build in intensity. Among those elements are also popular beliefs, often subliminal, that all people are *not* equal, that the murders of some people are more important events than the murders of others. That line of thinking even carries over into how news is covered. Sandy Pudar, assistant news director and former morning show executive producer at WGN-TV, used to oversee a six-hour block of news and entertainment Mondays through Fridays. She has seen thoughts about murder victims who are believed to be gang members travel full circle.

> [W]hen you realize that I started out as a young producer almost ten years ago, we had a very hard-and-fast rule here at WGN-TV—that I was taught, that we don't report gang murders. So, we would have overnight shootings and I would want to cover it—perhaps consider going there live—and the desk [assignment desk] would say no, no, no, no, it was a gang shooting, and we're not covering that. How interesting [that] ten years later, that's pretty much all we cover. And I mean it was a hard-and-fast rule that when there was a gang murder, we weren't even to touch the story, and now there are over five hundred murders in the city.[1]

Many times television news executives are conflicted about not being able to give equal treatment to all murder stories. Jennifer Lyons, news director at WGN-TV and CLTV, was an executive producer for years before going into management. She has witnessed unequal treatment given to murder victims.

> Are we aware? Yes. Can we cover everything right now? Violence is at epidemic proportions. Can we cover every single story knowing that our resources are limited? Websites are doing it [covering all murder stories]. They can do that because they have a different working model. We don't—we can't fill our newscast with a bunch of murders because, then, no one would watch. It would be too depressing. And we have to find a balance. But, are we aware that we choose certain stories? Murder should not happen to any person—any person anywhere. You know, I've been producing for a long time, and I've been sitting in that chair, deciding . . . and I sit there and say, should we cover the story? Should we not? And you do run through those checks and balances, and you do go for the stories that are interesting. But, at the same time there are many days when I step back and . . . it's not just another gangbanger, that's somebody's child.[2]

MURDER IN THE NEWS

Each year, in every major city across the country, there are hundreds of murder cases. But for the public most of the victims remain nameless fatalities of violence—victims they never hear about. On the other hand, the identities of a tiny percentage of those victims do become known, and in some cases, those casualties become so sensationalized that the deceased attain near-mythic status.

As an example: according to the *Chicago Tribune*, in Chicago in 2015, there were 468 murders compared with 416 the year before; a 12.5 percent increase. There were also 2,900 shootings (13 percent more than the year prior), up 29 percent since 2013.[3] Yet only around two hundred of those murders made the television news—the rest were ignored by other news organizations, which went on to take an even smaller group of victims and expand those stories. What happened to all the rest? Why did the other two hundred victims go unreported? In contrast, what was it about those two hundred cases that caused reporters to go talk to the victims' families and do follow-up reports if a suspect was arrested in the case?

In Chicago in February 2013, the case of fifteen-year-old Hadiya Pendleton, who was shot and killed by prowling street gang thugs who mistakenly thought she was standing with rival gang members, dominated the headlines for three weeks after she died.[4] First Lady Michelle Obama traveled to Chicago to attend Hadiya's funeral, along with the governor of Illinois, the mayor of Chicago, and other prominent civic leaders. Hadiya's story was discussed in the news for months thereafter. On the anniversary of her murder, all Chicago television stations revisited her case and did follow-up stories.

Take another example: in New York in August 1986, the brutal killing of eighteen-year-old Jennifer Levin came to be known as the Preppie Murder Case.[5] It monopolized television newscasts and tabloid newspapers in New York for two years.

Also in New York, in July 2011, an eight-year-old boy, Leiby Kletzky, was abducted off a Brooklyn street. The child, who was killed and dismembered, had been given a combination of drugs before he was smothered, according to the medical examiner.[6] Kletzky became lost after leaving a day camp. According to police, the boy asked a man, Levi Aron, for help. Surveillance cameras also showed the two together. Detectives later found the boy's severed feet, wrapped in plastic, in Aron's freezer. Authorities also found a cutting board and three bloody carving knives. A year later, Aron was sentenced to forty years to life in prison.

In Los Angeles, from January 1, 2007, to December 31, 2012—a five-year period—there were 1,668 murders.[7] However, only a few dozen of those crimes were front-page stories or led off the nightly news. But one case in particular captured worldwide attention: the murder investigation and trial of O. J. Simpson. The Simpson case dominated newscasts and was front-page material for weeks.

On the day Hadiya Pendleton was killed, at least two other people were murdered in Chicago—human beings whose names never made the headlines.[8] In fact, their deaths were ignored or overlooked by the local news media. But the families of those other two victims, nonetheless, grieved their loss and quietly suffered in anonymous loneliness.

One of the victims was twenty-seven-year-old Devin Common from the Greater Grand Crossing area on the South Side of Chicago.[9] The other victim was Gino Angotti, aged twenty. Angotti's sister, Vanessa Snyder, told me she was distraught that her brother's killer was still walking the streets.[10] Snyder said in Hadiya's case the intense public pressure, citywide manhunt, and $40,000 reward to find Hadiya's killers brought swift action in hunting down and charging two individuals: eighteen-year-old Michael Ward and twenty-year-old Kenneth Williams. But, in her brother's murder, she feels the case was largely unreported by the media and has meant that the people who robbed and killed Gino aren't feeling the same pressure.

The two men charged in Hadiya's murder had "the book thrown

at them": Michael Ward, the alleged shooter, was charged with 141 murder counts.[11] His attorney, Jeff Granich, said in a phone interview that he's never heard of a case of a single murder with anything close to that number of counts.[12]

The high-profile nature of the case, he said, appears to have led prosecutors to pile on the charges. "I know prosecutors want to show they're taking this case seriously," he said. "But the 141 counts have the opposite result: instead of looking professional and serious, they look silly and dumb."

Some of the attempted murder counts and other charges relate to Pendleton's friends who were in the park with her. But Granich said he still couldn't fathom how prosecutors ended up with so many counts. Former Chicago police superintendent Garry McCarthy says the shooter in Hadiya's case should never have been on the street:

> Hadiya Pendleton should be in school right now. But she's not because the alleged shooter in that case pled guilty to a gun possession, two months before [she was killed], and should not have been on the streets. Time and time again we are saying this. Last year at least 160 separate shootings were murders that could've been prevented, that we know about, if individuals were incarcerated instead of on the streets . . . after committing a crime of possession of a loaded firearm.[13]

When cases are sensationalized in news coverage they soar to the top of the public interest scale. As mentioned earlier, these "sensational" stories have certain "innate" elements about them that catch the attention of reporters and editors. It could simply be an item in the coroner's report that makes the case "stand out" from all the others. Or, it could be an insistent family member who refuses to let the case go quietly and who pesters reporters to do more digging into the case until a special nugget of information is found, upon which to hang the story. And once television news editors see the story with "more meat" than the usual nameless victim—and if it is a "slow news day"—a story that would have ordinarily been ignored could lead off the show and become fanned by incessant television coverage until the victims become familiar household names.

Two names that will forever be linked together are George Zimmerman and Trayvon Martin. The fatal shooting of Trayvon Martin, who was unarmed, by George Zimmerman took place on the night of February 26, 2012, in Sanford, Florida. Martin was a seventeen-year-old African American high school student. Zimmerman was a twenty-eight-year-old mixed-race Hispanic who was the neighborhood watch coordinator for the gated community where Martin was temporarily staying and where the shooting took place. Zimmerman was questioned by police for nearly five hours on the night of the shooting and then released.

It was at this point that the case was about to become lost in the shuffle of shootings and murders. But, little by little, the story began to gather momentum as Martin's family members refused to let the violent death go away. Additionally, the fact that Martin was unarmed and carrying a bag of Skittles and a soft drink became one of the hooks upon which the story was hung. Skittles, a seventeen-year-old kid killed for no apparent reason, and the fact that Martin was wearing a hoodie "clicked" with reporters and community groups. The story continued to grow. For six weeks the case gathered more energy until Zimmerman was rearrested and charged with murder.

Since Martin was killed while wearing a hoodie, hoodies were used as a sign of protest, and many cities staged "million hoodie marches" or "hundred hoodie marches." Additionally, some professional athletes, including Carmelo Anthony and the entire Miami Heat roster, tweeted photos of themselves wearing hoodies.[14]

Bags of Skittles candy and cans of Arizona Iced Tea were also used as protest symbols. Outside an African American barbershop in Evanston, Illinois, bags of Skittles were hung like decorations on a Christmas tree to honor Trayvon Martin.[15] (Martin was reported to be returning from a 7-Eleven convenience store with these items when he was shot, although the beverage he purchased was actually an Arizona brand fruit drink.)

Eventually George Zimmerman's side of the story began to be heard—that he and Martin had become entangled in a violent physical altercation resulting in injuries to Zimmerman's head. Zimmerman pled not guilty, claiming self-defense. Zimmerman's trial began on June 10, 2013, in Sanford, Florida. On July 13, 2013, a jury acquitted him of second-degree murder and of manslaughter charges.

The examples above are of victims who were unknown before they were killed. But when a prominent or high-profile individual is murdered, families of the victims are almost automatically assured that blaring headlines will trumpet the story and television newscasters will, agitatedly, announce breaking news with "team coverage."

MOURNING OF PROMINENT MURDER VICTIMS

In Western society in the last fifty years, television news has played a significant role in shaping how society determines who is prominent and, when it comes to murder, why he or she should be afforded preferential treatment. But this act of lauding some individuals more than others has always been the case.

Ancient folklore is filled with stories that deal with the murders of leaders, chiefs, kings, and other heads of clans or social groups. The demise of these "special" individuals was often followed by universal feelings of grief, apprehension, and profound loss. Over the millennia one dominant characteristic has been present in those who receive such adulation: they are *prominent* in the eyes of their social group.

I think of an imaginary figure like "Og, the Fire Keeper," a primitive caveman who knew the secret of starting and building a roaring campfire. If someone took his life, you can bet that members of Og's clan, sitting around a flickering fire in a cold, dark grotto, would spin tales of his hunting exploits—telling each other stories of how Og brought down his kill using his trusty atlatl and spear. His clan would marvel at how he amazingly started and built a fire so the fresh kill could be eaten and the rest preserved.

Strict rituals have evolved for mourning the murders of prominent people. Depending on the social group, various customs, beliefs, songs, dances, tales, spiritual sacrifices, and other traditions are common when a revered person is murdered and the funeral is held.

There is even a funeral company in Houston, Texas, that honors the lives and legacies of prominent individuals. LHT Consulting Group specializes in providing funeral and memorial consulting, master planning, and implementation of services to celebrate the lives of distinguished individuals. Their clients have been US presidents and first ladies, senators, Hollywood stars, members of Congress, professional athletes, and high-profile entertainers. Their funerals can cost several hundred thousand dollars.[16]

The services this company offers are way beyond the means of the average citizen. Yet, everyone will need some care and attention once he or she dies—it's the level of responsiveness that will differ: from dispassionate care in an anonymous pauper's grave to horse-drawn carriages taking the deceased to a multimillion-dollar mausoleum.

When these special, high-profile individuals die, journalists give them extra attention. There can be televised tributes and extensive coverage of the funerals and/or memorial services. Many times special editorial meetings are held so that producers can plan how the coverage of a mayor or cardinal or popular sports hero will be covered. Television stations will come together and forget their competitive differences so that everyone gets the same information. It's called pool coverage, and one station will provide a camera crew that supplies the video to everyone in town, given out on a pool feed and supplied to all the stations. Or the stations will divide up the coverage, with one supplying the inside pool camera, another providing a camera crew at another location, and so on. And if a high-profile person is murdered that just adds to the enormity of the coverage.

PERCEPTION VS. REALITY

In the United States today, the AC Nielsen Company, which surveys households, reports that 96 percent of homes have television sets.[17] This means that the vast majority of Americans are "fed" information selected and decided upon by someone else.

Ask most people in major cities across the country about crime and they will tell you that it is a growing problem, that murders are occurring with greater frequency today than, say, five or ten years ago. But that is not true—just the opposite is happening. Crime in the United States has been up and down. Over the past two decades, the United States has experienced an unpredicted drop in crime. Chicago, while often portrayed as the most violent city in the country, has seen sustained drops in violent crime and homicide rates during this time, but the decrease has recently stopped and rates have bounced back up again. According to a report released in December 2013, during a highly publicized press conference (by Chicago mayor Rahm Emanuel and former police superintendent Garry McCarthy), Chicago—like other US cities—experienced a significant decline in overall crime and violent crime. Levels of violent crime three years ago were in fact at their lowest rates in four decades.[18] (But it should be noted that during the writing of this book murder rates in 2016 were the highest in more than twenty years. In fact, a story on CNN's website reports, "Chicago's 500th homicide of the year happened over Labor Day weekend, according to the *Chicago Tribune*. That number carries a lot of weight for the city—not just in quantity, but in meaning: 2016 is now the deadliest year in two decades."[19])

The 2013 city press conference had been held to announce a drop in murders, but it was contradicted three years later when crime spiked, indicating that the pendulum of violence was quickly swinging back and forth. The earlier report ran "against the grain" of common belief, so much so that reporters attending the press conference questioned whether the numbers had been "doctored" to show the city in a favorable light. (I also attended that press conference and observed the questions of reporters as they attempted to discredit or uncover specious or distorted data in the literature.) As it turns out, the report, by a team from Yale University, was factual: the data was accurate. Even so, the perception by the public is that crime is a growing menace and violent activities are creeping into every neighborhood. In reality, our awareness of events in our surroundings is more acute today than ever before; news reports, Twitter posts, and Facebook chatter inundate us constantly with positive and negative information. News information is available twenty-four hours a day, allowing viewers to access any information they seek.

TELEVISION NEWS DECISION MAKERS

In every television news department there are individuals (producers and assignment editors) who have the responsibility for deciding which stories or events will be included in each newscast. But what factors motivate these individuals to decide that, for instance, the murder of one person is more significant than the murder of another? Pat Curry, planning editor at WGN-TV, sat at the assignment desk for many years. He thinks many elements come into play when the gatekeepers in the newsrooms—the assignment editors—

begin to filter all the shootings and other crimes that pour into a big-city newsroom:

> Let's say if it [shooting] occurs on the South Side—and [the] majority of our crimes have been—is it necessarily not a story? No—there are criteria and the criteria might be: How long will I spend on the phone with the person who is telling me the story? Or, how much do they know? In other words, if this is a personal story, is it one of innocence? I'm trying to establish that. I don't care [where] it happens—North Side, South Side, West Side—but obviously geography does play a big part in how we cover crime—[a] big part.[20]

In Chicago—once called one of the most segregated cities in America, based on US Census Bureau data stretching back to 1890[21]—African American neighborhoods on the "West" and "South" Sides of the city have become "code." Simply saying, "a shooting happened on the South Side" infers that black people were involved in the incident. Likewise, a crime in Humboldt Park means a Puerto Rican was involved; Little Village means the actors were Mexican; North Side or suburban presupposes white people. So, producers and editors need only refer to neighborhood "areas" to avoid mentioning ethnic groups by name.

Television stations are commercial enterprises. Their success depends, to a great degree, on how many viewers are watching television and, more importantly, which station they are watching. Viewer preferences are determined by ratings.

In recent years some television stations have achieved high ratings by concentrating on murders and other mayhem. Critics of this type of programming call it "sensationalism" and "cheap." But sensationalism attracts viewers, viewers raise ratings, high ratings draw advertisers, and advertisers write the checks that keep the stations in business. (The Super Bowl is a good example of a program with high ratings that charges advertisers astronomical prices for precious ad time during the program. Advertisers during the 2014 Super Bowl paid $4 million for a thirty-second commercial. In the 2016 Super Bowl a thirty-second spot during CBS's broadcast went for $5 million, according to the network's CEO Leslie Moonves in an earnings call last year, as *Fortune* reported.[22])

If viewers didn't watch popular or sensational programs, stations would drop the shows as soon as the ratings numbers began to fall. However, viewers do watch them. So stations respond by covering more turmoil and sensationalism. Some cable shows, for instance, rely on nothing but sensationalistic material. Likewise, most news programs fill the first segment of the show with stories of death and destruction—i.e., murders, fires, car crashes, and other havoc. They also try to include "soft" human interest stories like "Twiggy the Water-Skiing Squirrel," which was a big hit on our news. Producers who place stories on the WGN-TV web page know exactly which stories will do well, based on previous postings. Web producer Elyse Russo says,

> [C]ertainly anything that has animals is going to do well—bottom line, it's going to do great. But, I will say, sometimes the education stories and city hall stories will get good traffic when it's a hot-button issue. Also, if it's the CPS [Chicago Public Schools] school closure or even the littering ban—if they talk about that. City hall . . . a lot of people had things to say about that, or even the plastic bags [whether Chicago should ban plastic bags]—a lot of people are clicking through. Maybe it's not going to do as good as crime stories, which do well—but, if it's a murder and we have a photo of the victim, and good interviews with relatives or witnesses, to go with stories—it will do very well.[23]

Producers say they're just giving viewers what they want. And herein lies a key question: do implicit or unspoken notions of the audience play a role in the decisions of producers and editors to give greater news coverage to prominent victims of murder than to those victims who have little or no notoriety? That is one of the questions we will explore in this book as we examine the workings of television newsrooms and the decisions that are made when deciding which stories of murder victims to cover and which ones to disregard.

Before going any further it is important to define several terms so there is no misunderstanding when certain language is used to label job descriptions and vernacular common to most newsrooms.

TERMS

PRODUCER: The person who is responsible for the content and "style" of the newscast. The producer decides the order and length of stories in the newscast, giving top-story status to events based upon the producer's judgment or "news savvy."

ASSIGNMENT EDITOR: The key person in the newsroom who has the responsibility for monitoring police and fire radios, taking phone tips from viewers, reading press releases, and assigning reporters and camera crews to news events. The assignment editors are "first-line gatekeepers" as they make the judgment decision as to what news events are ignored and which ones are brought to the attention of the producers.

REPORTER/ANCHOR: News personnel who appear on camera delivering or reporting the news. Anchors report the news from the television studio. Reporters deliver the news from "live," on-the-spot locations or record stories on videotape or digitally to be played on the air at a later time. Field reporters exercise news judgment when assessing conditions or the "worth" of stories once they're on the scene.

RATINGS: A sampling method for determining when and how many viewers are watching a particular television station and for how long. Broadcasters and advertisers make decisions—what shows to run and when, what commercials to buy—based on ratings. According to AC Nielsen's website,

> The Nielsen Ratings are coupled with detailed analysis of consumer viewing behavior and demographic information. Which members of a household are watching which shows? And which programs do they all watch together? Which family characteristics, such as pet ownership, income and education correlate with viewing choices? This depth of knowledge allows clients to refine their campaigns based on demographics, day-part and audience composition.[24]

TOP STORY: The first story in a newscast. This report is placed at the beginning of the show because it is deemed the most "important" story in the program. Producers "stack" each show so that an important or significant story leads off each segment.

BREAKING NEWS: News stories that occur without notice or in a surprising manner are termed breaking news. Murders, fires, natural disasters, or other uncommon events fall into this category.

With these terms understood we can begin to examine several questions that will form the basis of the analysis throughout this book:

1. What makes a particular murder important as producers plan the placement and construction of the news program?
2. How do television news producers and editors decide which murders are worth covering and which ones are not?
3. Do television news producers have a tacit or understood image of which murder victims they "think" the audience is interested in learning more about?
4. Is the "prominence," or lack thereof, of the victim a determining factor in the coverage of murder victims?
5. What are the implicit notions of the audience (young, old,

male, female) that have an impact on the coverage and selection of murder victims?

6. Do producers and editors think of the audience when they
   shape the "meanings" ascribed to traditional news values and
   elevate the importance of some murder victims over others?
7. What role does the audience image play as the producer begins
   stacking or building each segment of the news program?
8. How do the variables of the victim's race, gender, age, and
   socioeconomic level affect how he or she will be treated in the
   news?

MARKETING THE NEWS PRODUCT

What is the reason television news leaders have decided that chasing
murder stories is an effective manner for drawing in viewers? If we
look at a typical television news program, it is easier to dissect if we
examine it from a promotional or marketing perspective. In modern
news organizations, it is fair to presume that an audience must, in
some way, be lured or attracted. Promos, teases, headline blurbs,
and other devices are often used to appeal to viewers to watch news
programs. In other words, "audience" must clearly be factored into
the news production formula. The audience is still a key consideration, albeit often tacitly, "as a given" factored into news judgments,
technologies, and procedures. Retired WGN-TV news director Greg
Caputo is a well-known and highly respected journalist. He has been
working in television for over forty years—thirty years as a news
director overseeing newsrooms in large metropolitan cities. Caputo
says about WGN's audience,

> Yes, I do have a vision of the audience, but not necessarily as the
> audience of consumers, but rather as an audience desiring infor-
> mation in order to go about their daily lives. In addition, I have in

my mind, of the audience—[it] is me. It's hard for me to put myself in somebody else's shoes. So, I can't sit here and say, oh yes, I see a group of people out there who are twenty-five years old, and all women, and all white. I can identify with that—I can communicate with that—but I don't know what the audience wants. So, I've tried to put into shows, when I was a producer, as best I could, stuff that interested me. And I think I'm average enough that that kind of works—and I think it sort of works. . . . As a news director, I've tried to instill in the newscasts, stories, or crusades, or other important issues that interest me. They interest me because I think they are important. They interest me because I think they're fun. They interest me because I think it's something different.[25]

It is understood through perceptions of the audience that there is an interest in murder victims. Those insights are part of the overall "construction" of news. This is one of the prime considerations to remember as we examine the impact of the audience on news preparation and the development of a show.

I believe that news workers are conscientiously concerned with creating the best news product they can: stories, features, weather, sports, and other segments within the newscasts. Their objective is to "make" the best news product they know how. Murders are often prominent news stories. Not all murders are given identical news "value"; most are not covered, others are given marginal attention, and some attain "headline" or special coverage in a newscast. It is within this context that editors and producers go about selecting stories, trying to appeal to the audience they hope will be watching.

News executives like Jennifer Lyons are using web analytics to help them gather a clear profile of their viewers:

So many people are getting their news from Twitter. . . . So many kids these days don't watch TV. So, when they get up in the morning and they hear about Justin Bieber standing on the Blackhawks logo—

what pops up is where they get their information from. They're not as loyal to a certain television station. And so, our content needs to be on the web . . . but it also needs to be somewhere where people turn on the TV and sit and watch. TVs aren't going away—they are here to stay. And I think people sit in their living rooms and watch TV. But, on a daily basis, information—between Twitter and Facebook and just plain "old school"—people are getting their news that way too.[26]

Lyons is correct, and the next focus of this chapter looks at perceptions of the audience from those same three levels of analysis: individual, organizational, and institutional.

RECOGNIZING NEWS

Everyone has an idea of what's news and what isn't. Much of the understanding of the audience is bound up within the product image of the news. That understanding is an example of tacit or unstated knowledge—a gut feeling. Although such knowledge is often difficult to articulate, it is very real and does help shape the news product throughout the news organization.

Many people have tried to define the term "news." The answers are as varied as the people who are asked to give a definition.

> *When a dog bites a man, that is not news, but when a man bites a dog, that is news.*
> —Leo Rosten, political scientist and author

> *Anything that makes the reader say, "Gee Whiz!"*
> —Arthur McEwen, *San Francisco Examiner* editorial writer

SECOND-RATE MURDERS . . . REALLY?

Good news isn't news. Bad news is news.

—Henry Luce, founder of *Time*

News is the exceptional, something which threatens, benefits, outrages, enlightens, titillates, or amuses.

—Mort Rosenblum, special correspondent
for the Associated Press

Hey, Martha, take the meat loaf out of the oven and look at this.

—Arthur Lord, NBC
WGN-TV news director Greg Caputo
has a more pragmatic definition of news:

I once used to work for a guy . . . in Pittsburgh, an anchorman who would quite boastfully say, "News is what I say it is." And I used to think how arrogant that was. I used to think it was a terrible thing. But the older I got and the more I analyzed that . . . the more I realized that that's exactly what news is. News *is* what I say it is because to every person that watches a newscast: when they pick on the judgment [complain] of putting that story in the newscasts at all, their comment is, "That's not news. What's the matter with you? That's not news." But, what they are trying to say is: that's not news to me. And I'm saying, obviously, because I put it in a newscast, that that's news to me. So, to a certain extent, we all believe that—news is what I say it is.[27]

Caputo has made a brilliant revelation. While journalists are probably reluctant to admit it, news *is* what they decide it is. If not, certain stories wouldn't be covered—the decision to go after one story instead of another is made several times along the "news production" assembly line.

Assignment editors, reporters, and producers must all agree that the story is worth covering or it can be killed at any point before the story ever makes it on the air.

In television newsrooms, several times a day, decisions are made on what is news and what isn't. Many times those decisions determine what will air and what won't, what the audience will see and hear and what it will not. Consequently, the newsperson's perception of the audience and what the audience is interested in helps to form decisions about what's news. As Bill Kovach and Tom Rosenstiel write in their book, *The Elements of Journalism: What Newspeople Should Know and the Public Should Expect,* there are some clear principles that journalists in a democratic society agree on and that citizens have a right to expect:

- Journalism's first obligation is to the truth.
- Its first loyalty is to citizens.
- Its essence is a discipline of verification.
- Its practitioners must maintain an independence from those they cover.
- Journalism must serve as an independent monitor of power.
- It must provide a forum for public criticism and compromise.
- It must strive to make the significant interesting and relevant.
- It must keep the news comprehensive and proportional.
- Its practitioners must be allowed to exercise their personal conscience.[28]

According to the Chicago Police Department, in the city of Chicago the number of murders fluctuates from year to year, between a low of three hundred to four hundred, during some years, to a high in 1974 of 970 murders in that violent year.[29] Yet television stations report a small percentage of those cases. Some of those murders receive "top-story" or even "team" coverage (where several reporters cover separate facets of the same story). Other murders may receive only a mention.

Let's examine this situation. Suppose an assignment editor was presented with several murder stories to cover. And suppose there was only one reporter in the station at that time. If only one story had to be selected out of the following five, which one would you choose: a person shot with a handgun, a victim shot with a rifle, a person stabbed to death with a knife, a person killed with a baseball bat, or a teen who chased and killed a woman with a poisoned dart from a blowgun?

I can tell you right away that the reporter would be sent on the story dealing with the blow dart victim. And if I could receive your feedback, the majority of you would say that the editor was correct in selecting that story. Why? Because the manner of death was very unusual, causing the viewers to want to know more. Even when the crime doesn't result in a death, the manner of the case is what causes journalists to salivate.

It is safe to say that in the city of Chicago, on any given day, there are scores of stabbings, cuttings, slicings, gougings, and all manners of people being cut with knives and sharp objects. Those cases never get covered in the news. But in August 2013 when two longtime neighbors, who were good friends, got into an argument and one man came after the other with a chainsaw, the story became headline news and appeared in the first segment of most newscasts. Days later a follow-up story appeared in the *Chicago Sun-Times*. Reportedly, the two men got into a dispute over money, and one of the friends alleg-edly cut the other man's ear and fingers with the chainsaw.[30]

Because the attack was unusual, reporters jumped all over the story and followed the case all the way through the criminal justice system—something that doesn't even happen with many murder stories.

Likewise when African American teens, riding the elevated trains (CTA) in Chicago, began snatching cell phones from passengers as they were getting off trains, the stories became hot news. One vic-tim's death became a front-page story when one of the teens shoved a woman down the steps of a train station while attempting to escape with someone's cell phone.[31]

Defendants in many of these high-profile cases received swift and stinging justice from the courts because of the surge of snatch-and-grab robberies targeting public transit riders' new electronic gadgets, which can quickly bring hundreds of dollars on the black market. Yet, these stories may have saved some riders from being mugged by alerting them to a potential danger of burying their heads in their smartphones and being oblivious to their surroundings.

The audience itself has come to know, understand, and accept what news workers choose to feed it. Viewers are seldom outraged enough to write the station. And even if they disagree with what they have just seen, they often continue watching the same channel and the same news program time after time.[32]

That sad story of an innocent victim losing her life in such a senseless manner touched viewers and readers in Chicago. And, like Hadiya Pendleton's story, when there was intense pressure from the press to solve the case, justice was swift and a suspect was arrested and charged four months later.

THE POWERFUL IMPACT OF HEADLINE STORIES

When editors reflect on the interest of the audience, on years when murder rates are high, television stations tend to report on more murder cases. On years when the murder rate is lower, news teams report on more human interest stories and other "softer" news. It still is not clear if this is a case of the tail wagging the dog or not. But more murders occurring in the city of Chicago does seem to dictate that attention will be given to more murder stories, resulting in greater coverage—while fewer murders per year result in a decrease in murder stories on the air.[33]

News executives are aware of percentages of stories that are hard news and softer features. WGN-TV news director Jennifer Lyons says,

> I think we're more aware than we were years ago. I think we've come full circle, and I think part of the problem is that there are so many murders, now, that we really are paying attention because it's a problem and we have to fix the problem. So, I think that we're paying attention more. Do we have the resources to cover more? No. Do other people? Yes. Other types of news outlets—yes. Are we paying attention more? I think we are. Could we pay attention more—make better decisions? We could. And, we aren't always going to know the real, full story—we just aren't.[34]

A better question to answer would be, does the increased pressure from more television stories dealing with murders result in greater, more focused attention by the police department to stop the shootings and reduce public pressure? Police will tell you they work just as hard trying to solve *all* murders. Retired first deputy superintendent of the Chicago Police Department Al Wysinger says they look upon all murders with the same critical eye:

> We don't necessarily get blowback. . . . [A]s much as people find it hard to believe, we try to treat each and every case as an individual case—no matter who the victim is, we just want to try and go out there and bring solace to the families of the victims.
>
> Unfortunately, these high-profile cases sometimes do bring pressure, but we try not to make that a reason why we go the extra mile—to make sure that these cases are cleared up.[35]

But there is a difference sometimes in how police view a case. Regrettably, some murder cases are viewed by police as just some "more ghetto mess," or police pass matters to the bottom of the stack for other reasons.[36]

Occasionally police commanders get phone calls from city hall when a high-profile murder is in the news (Chicago mayor Rahm Emanuel has a reputation for being brutal in his behind-the-scenes dealings with subordinates[37]). Cops will tell you one thing—"shit rolls downhill." Those commanders who get an earful from the mayor "chew out" their captains and lieutenants who, in turn, point their fingers at the sergeants and detectives, who pass on stern warnings and retaliations toward the rank-and-file "grunt officers." The patrol officers shake up their informants and put pressure on other miscreants and reprobates, making everyone's life miserable. And if there is a substantial monetary reward, on top of the ongoing pressure, the suspect has a *less than zero* chance of staying out of the clutches of the law. Somebody will turn him in—even his own grandmother.

CONVICT FIRST, CHECK FOR GUILT LATER

When journalists make a decision to go hard on a story and cover it "like a rug," there are bound to be reactions. The press is powerful. High-profile murder cases create tremendous pressure on police and city officials to solve the crimes. Unfortunately, the overwhelming need to find the murderer can corrupt the judicial process. In Chicago during a nineteen-year period, making arrests and gaining convictions—at any cost—took priority over abiding by the law.

The name Jon Burge (Chicago police commander, 1972–1991) still evokes chilling memories of a horrible time in the history of the Chicago Police Department. The former commander and detective, now a convicted felon, gained notoriety for allegedly torturing more than two hundred criminal suspects—nearly all black—between 1972 and 1991, in order to force confessions.[38] The accusations are like something out of a wartime prison camp: electric shock and cattle prods, near suffocation with a typewriter bag, mock executions with a pistol, and beatings with telephone books.

Burge was able to carry on this type of behavior because those around him turned their heads and said nothing. His actions were well known but whispered about by his fellow police officers. Many knew about the deplorable but common practices that occurred during the 1960s and 1970s. Eventually, stories about Burge began to gain credence as more and more convicted felons tried to get someone to listen to their frightening, unbelievable stories of torture and being forced to confess to crimes they did not commit.[39]

On January 11, 2011, Burge was found guilty and sentenced to four and a half years in prison for lying under oath. It brought to a close a horrible case of torture, discrimination, and abuse of power that ruined countless lives—not in the name of justice—just to lower the statistical data on crime. But no crimes were actually solved because the real criminals were still on the loose committing more crimes and running up statistics. As of this writing, the city of Chicago has paid out around $100 million in restitution to the innocent men who went to prison as a result of the torture by Burge (that figure continues to grow).[40]

The Burge case *is* significant because news gatekeepers were quick to believe a union police spokesperson or police PR person before they would a citizen who accused a police captain of misconduct. But once Burge was formally charged, decades later, TV stations went after Burge with a vengeance. Assignment editors sent reporters chasing Burge all the way from his Chicago house to his Florida hideout.[41] The commander who once had near-total freedom decades ago to ruin the lives of countless African American men who had been snatched off the street was now a pariah within his own police department.

How stations choose to cover murder stories is an example of *tacit* knowledge. Ponder this question: which should get more coverage—a hurricane in Honduras that kills hundreds of people or the disappearance of a six-year-old child beauty queen named JonBenet Ramsey? Cultural prejudices often influence the decision. Most Americans would be more interested in what happened to JonBenet than hundreds of foreigners in a country that many people couldn't locate on a map.

So local media attention will focus on the single child over the hundreds of faceless casualties in another country. This same bias can be seen in the reporting of murder victims. Black-on-black crime, especially in poor areas, receives little coverage. But if that same per- petrator chooses a white victim, the coverage will make a big "news splash." This fuels cultural prejudice and alters the public's percep- tion of reality. But it is not entirely a racial determination.

If a black teenaged gang member was shot and killed in most major cities, his death probably wouldn't make the news—unless there were unusual circumstances. But take that same black kid and put some textbooks under his arm and have him walking to school when he's shot, and the TV stations would have helicopters in the sky over the scene: same kid, same crime, different perceptions.

If a white female was shot and killed in Chicago on Michigan Avenue—the Magnificent Mile shopping district—again, there'd be helicopters in the sky. Take that same woman and place her in the "hillbilly" section of town and she might slip through the cracks: same woman, same crime, different perceptions.

Murders in Chicago peaked first in 1974, with 970 murders when the city's population was over three million, resulting in a murder rate of around twenty-nine per 100,000, and again in 1992, with 943 murders when the city had *fewer* than three million people, resulting in a murder rate of thirty-four per 100,000.[42]

With a murder rate so high—almost three every day—something interesting happened at assignment desks around the city. When the murder rate was much lower editors would dispatch camera crews and roll out the door on each death; each one was considered news-worthy. But when the murder rate skyrocketed and an alarm would come in for a single murder somewhere in the city—unless there were more of the compelling elements that we will discuss later in this book—editors, most of the time, did not assign a reporter unless the body count was larger.

Often, editors would sardonically joke, "We don't roll unless you've at least got two dead." Of course they didn't mean that literally, but in reality, with so many things going on and resources spread so thin, two dead or three dead would be necessary to spark the attention of news editors on most busy days.

Following 1992, the murder count in Chicago slowly decreased to 641 in 1999. In 2002, Chicago had a fewer number of murders but a significantly higher murder rate than New York or Los Angeles (these are per-person figures). In 2012 there were 506 homicides in Chicago—almost half the all-time high of 1974 when there were 970 murders. Yet, Chicago was characterized in national headlines as the murder capital of the country.[43] A more pejorative name also took hold when rap artists dubbed Chicago "Chi-raq," a city with more murders than wartime Iraq.[44]

Chapter Two

MURDER COVERAGE AS A REFLECTION OF SOCIETY

I t is rare that a veteran "general assignment" reporter is shocked to the core by what he or she discovers while covering a news story. After a couple of decades of reporting on fires, floods, multiple murders, drug cases, revenge killings, drive-by gang shootings, and even the unsettling evil perpetrated on children by perverts, not much will make a seasoned reporter step back and say, "Well, damn, I can't believe that! Wow!"

But such was the case on November 16, 1995. By that time I had been reporting for almost twenty-five years, and not much was new to me. My cameraman and I were sent outside Chicago to far west suburban Addison, Illinois, to cover a multiple murder.

Soon after arriving, we began to put the grizzly pieces of the story together. Jacqueline Williams, her boyfriend Fedell Caffey, and her cousin Laverne Ward entered the home of Ward's ex-girlfriend, twenty-eight-year-old Deborah Evans.[1]

Deborah, who was nine months pregnant—presumably with Ward's child—had three children: ten-year-old Samantha, eight-year-old Joshua, and nineteen-month-old Jordan. Jordan was believed to be Ward's son.

Deborah had a restraining order against Ward for domestic violence but allowed the group into her home, anyway. Once inside, Ward tried to make Deborah accept $2,000 in exchange for her soon-to-be-born baby. When she refused, Caffey pulled out a gun and shot her. Then, Ward and Caffey hunted down Deborah's daughter Samantha and stabbed her to death.

The three returned to Deborah, who was still alive. Using scissors and a knife, they extracted the unborn male fetus from her womb, performed mouth-to-mouth resuscitation on him, then cleaned him in the kitchen sink and dressed him. Deborah, of course, died an unimaginably painful and horrible death.

As the reporter on that story, I tried to give viewers some perspective about Deborah's murder and just how difficult it would have been to perform what was nothing more than a crude, rudimentary Caesarian section on a dying woman and still be able to deliver the baby—alive. I decided to use my past military medical experience to explain to the audience what had taken place in that house of horrors.

While serving in the US Army, I had worked as a medic and was trained as an operating room assistant. I had worked on countless deliveries and hundreds of Caesarian sections on wives of servicemen. So, during my live shot, I described to viewers what it is like to slice through the layers of the abdomen and into the uterus and how careful, even, a trained doctor must be to avoid wounding the baby inside the uterus, pressed up against the uterine wall. I talked about the cutting of the umbilical cord and the resuscitation of the baby and how lucky this child was to be alive. I also put into perspective how cold-blooded, brutal, and cruel the merciless killers must have been to have conceived of such an unbelievably heinous crime.

My report that evening gave viewers a firsthand, vivid, and at times chilling understanding of what had taken place in the apartment and what the last few agonizing moments for the victim, Deborah Evans, must have been like. The television station received dozens and dozens of phone calls from viewers who applauded our coverage, praised my reporting, and thanked us for explaining what had happened in such a clear and understandable manner.

All the while I was giving my report, I was thinking of my audience. I'm not the least bit squeamish, but I had just watched veteran police offers and seasoned detectives hurry out of the apartment and vomit on the grass outside the building. I, too, had just been mortified by the events I had discovered and wanted to give my television audience an idea of the magnitude—the butchery—of these brutal, disgusting, cold-blooded murders. But I also had to rein in and modify my descriptive manner to keep from offending viewers: too much detailed and graphic information could offend young or sensitive viewers and turn them off.

As a reporter, my job is to give the viewer an accurate description of the events I am covering, and that may mean using props, anecdotes, examples, and other tools at my disposal. Yet television news in 2017 is much different than what it was decades ago. It has morphed several times into an almost-instant presentation of stories that crystallize daily life in the cities where the television stations are located. This is how stations localize their news to amplify the appeal of the story.

When reporting on the murder of Deborah Evans, I called upon my experience as an army medic to give the audience a better understanding of the unbelievable events that had occurred in that house. I was able to personalize the story and draw in viewers, bringing them in closer to the story, by offering them information they could relate to and understand. Other reporters, no matter how well they wrote or how smoothly they talked, couldn't take their audience where I had taken mine—inside the "slaughter house" to clearly understand the details—where a fiendish "wild bunch" had been and was, now, on the loose.

MURDER: THE PERFECT BREAKING NEWS STORY

There are two major kinds of reports that make up each newscast: breaking news and planned stories. In every city in America, *breaking news* stories are basically the same: fires, shootings, major crimes, weather calamities, crashes (car, plane, train, and other vehicles), plus disasters—natural and human-made. Planned stories are all the rest that are assigned days before or at the last minute.

As reporters, we know which "special" stories to highlight in our specific locales. Planned stories differ from region to region across the country as local priorities determine what is important or unusual in that community: a county fair in Des Moines, Iowa; a rodeo in Casper, Wyoming; a back-to-school parade in Chicago; or high school football practice in Odessa, Texas. Each report would have special significance on the local channels, and viewers would find the stories especially appealing.

How the reporter builds the story (interviews used and video shown) and how she focuses her writing could clearly slant the story to have an outcome the reporter desires. Journalists deal with that reality each day and try to avoid that uneven coverage. That's why an effort is made to "balance" the report by including an opposing side of the story—if there is one.

There is no other side to a murder story. The universal conclusion is that murder is bad, wrong, and depraved—even putting someone out of his or her misery (i.e., euthanasia) is illegal in most US states.[2] No one would say it was okay to cut the Evans baby out of his mother's womb.

That's why murder stories—when they break—are for the most part pretty simple to cover and report. It is after more details come in that the motives and conflicts and other elements behind the story make it much more complicated to explain. For example, it was later revealed, during her trial, that Williams wanted a baby of her own and had planned to "pretend" the Evans baby was hers. A *Chicago Tribune* story gave more details, reporting, "Prosecutors said Williams faked her own pregnancy—complete with baby shower and a bogus birth certificate—in a plot to steal Evans' baby."[3]

So what goes through the mind of an assignment editor when an alert comes in notifying the desk that a murder victim has just been discovered? One of the first questions asked is, where did the murder take place? This simple inquiry has monumental implications. If the murder occurred on the South or West Side of Chicago, there is a 95 percent chance that the victim would be African American. If the victim was found on the North Shore in a leafy suburb, most likely the victim would be white. Would where the murder occurred make a difference in how quickly a camera crew was dispatched? WGN-TV managing editor Pat Curry says yes:

> Where is it? And, how many? That's pretty much it. Because when it comes down to it, we've got to make a lot of decisions during the day. . . .
>
> My initial thought is find out the basic information that the reporter [will need to know]. . . . Yes, where is it, who is it, and when did it happen? Flush out those details so I will have a firm idea in my mind.[4]

Where the murder occurred is important because if the crime was in an African American neighborhood and involved gang members, the victims would slide lower on the "importance scale" than if the murder involved a resident of an affluent suburb where fewer or no shootings were happening. You can call it racism or you can call it chasing stories that are not the norm, that are more unusual. Later in the book we will learn that because of the Internet, positive changes are occurring. Some news outlets are now making a more aggressive effort to balance out the coverage of murders all over the city.

Another assignment editor, Kelly Barnicle, adds another important component that prompts coverage:

> Age would be the very first [factor]. If it's a child, I think you [cover it]—that's a no-brainer. Yes, I would say age and maybe gender, and location, location, location. . . . If it's a fifteen-year-old in Chicago as opposed to Montgomery, Illinois (an hour outside Chicago), we might not make it there—I hate to say that. A lot of times we pressed further, over the circumstances—what else happened? It's a lot of things. It's the availability of crews—so it's not necessarily fair. What is news on the weekends is not necessarily news during the week and vice versa. Which is not a fair way to cover it—but that's what happens.[5]

Either way, as the data shows in the qualitative study undertaken in chapter four, the shooting in the suburb would get the attention while the West Side murder might go overlooked because so many of the shootings in Chicago are between rival gang members—people who are looked upon as the "bad guys" in the system. And assignment editors are quick to say they just don't hear about everything. Many of the crimes never reach the gatekeepers. Curry says,

> I can't call the police and say, "Hey, you got any murders?" It doesn't work that way. We have to hear about them. They have to be documented. So, we have to have a tip—so the person who's calling and is giving us information is the way we're finding [out]. And I'll say, "Thank you for telling me. Tell me more. What were the circumstances? Where were they shot? How old were they? What were the circumstances?" That caller becomes your source, and all of a sudden, things can change. So, it's not that we ignored [the murder]—we didn't hear about it.[6]

And it should be mentioned that once reporters are assigned to the murder story, most dive into the job with equal enthusiasm regardless of the victim's race. The filtering comes before and after the reporter has done the story. Either a decision is made not to cover the story, or after the report is in house the story gets shoved down in the show to the second or third segment or is dropped entirely (these are producer decisions). WGN-TV assistant news director Sandy Pudar says,

> If you can't get families to talk, if you can't get neighbors to talk, you have to move on . . . and how do you tell the story of someone if the family still won't cooperate? For instance, we're covering, right now, the murder of two people this morning, and the families don't want to talk and [aren't] releasing any pictures, and our reporters are hearing that there might be some gang involvement, so here are two men who'd just died and we will not know very much about them because the families are scared, and the community is scared, and it really hinders so much—you can't cover a story . . . and sometimes you just have to move on. And a lot of these names and faces just go unrecognized.[7]

These are "backstage" adjustments the producer has to make while covering a story, announcements that the public never hears about. Often stories fall apart because unforeseen elements disrupt and prevent the planned development of the story. Sometimes, no matter how hard a reporter may try to advance and expand a story, unseen forces or bad luck can derail the process, and the story is dropped.

But sometimes, something as simple as families or neighbors of victims being so determined to have the story investigated can and does make a difference in how that victim is covered. People who don't take no for an answer and who continue to prod reporters and desk editors usually get results. Ava Thompson Greenwell uses the Hadiya Pendleton case as a teaching tool for her journalism students:

So let's take Hadiya Pendleton, for example. She's one of those students who got a huge amount of coverage, right? And rightly so—at the same time I don't think she would've gotten that kind of coverage had she not been a good student, had she not just come from the inauguration of [the] president—and had a two-parent household—all those things that we value and say are critical to growing up. I think that's one of the reasons she got as much coverage as she did. And I think that timing, too, was a factor—that it came as close as it did on the heels of the inauguration was also a factor.[8]

But because the Internet is more individualized, web producers don't care as much about where the victim was from (location or race). Web producers have so much space to fill that almost any murder that comes to their attention will get posted. And it is on the web that viewer comments reveal the darker side of people's prejudices. Web producer Marisa Rodriguez explains, "Just this morning a teen was shot by a playground—I mean, that's headline magic. . . . It's those key words—playground, school, student—that really affect people. And I feel like [the term] gangbanger—turns them off. And that's when you get the comments, 'Well he deserved it,' and nasty things like that. You know?"[9]

By describing some stories as "headline magic," researchers have often pointed to the variety of concerns that help shape the news product, that help select which information is included in the news and how that information is treated. The tacit manner in which murder victims are selected for news coverage is an excellent example of the seemingly arbitrary process that takes place. In fact, it is an implicit modus operandi that follows a prescribed course of "gut feelings." An analysis of the scholarly work on the "construction" of news can be divided any number of ways. WGN-TV news director Jennifer Lyons knows which stories will do well on the web page and which could later be covered on Channel 9 News. So, she's careful to consider a mixture:

I think the biggest thing—we know what stories do well on the web, but we still have to provide the news for the Chicago area and for anyone else who wants to know what's going on in Chicago. So, the local school story is just as important as the water-skiing squirrel story. We may get more viewers on [the squirrel], but at the same time our job as content providers . . . [is to] provide both the local news and reputable content—and [also] in the trivial, fun stories that people click on. So, I think there's a fine balance that people are doing.[10]

Once I'm given an assignment, as I head to the minicam truck (the news van containing all of the editing and communications equipment), I'm already thinking of the elements that will be needed to tell the story. Having covered thousands of murders during my career, I already have a good idea what I will find at the scene; although that too has changed over the years.

In the 1970 and 1980s, when news crews arrived at the murder scene, you could walk right up to the door of a house where the killing occurred. Enterprising photographers would sometimes slip in the back door while the police were inside to get a shot of the victim and the bloody scene.

We knew many of the police officers by name or, certainly, by sight after seeing them over and over again at different murders. And if we didn't know the cops, they knew us because we were the ones on the air. I can't remember how many times a cop whispered in my ear details about a murder case that no one else knew. These were the days when a "news scoop" mattered to your boss and beating another channel on the air with a juicy detail would get you a strong "atta boy" back at the office.

During those years, if we got to the scene late, after police had taken control of the area (a time way before yellow police tape), we would have to stay until the body was "bagged and tagged" and wheeled into a waiting police wagon or the medical examiner's car. That would be the shot viewers would see on the evening news.

Today, crews usually don't get within a couple of blocks of the crime scene. Police block off an area with yellow tape to keep crews out. Even using a "telephoto lens" won't get you in sight of the victim. So, today we use helicopters to get the shots the reporter needs, bypassing the yellow tape and getting a close-up view from a mile away in the sky. Many stations also have camera operators who can operate drones, flying over the scene to get the shots the news team needs. We do what we have to do to tell the story the best way we can.

Some researchers have argued that the attitudes of individual journalists are not important; what *is* important are the stories they construct, which, by and large, do not bear out a "liberal" bias. Other research has suggested that journalists really are not liberal by nature but are more or less apolitical—tied instead to professional values. Even so, because there are so many steps to getting a story on the air, mistakes do happen. Retired news director Greg Caputo explains,

> There's two or three things I think every news director stays up at night over, and I think that's one of them—the filtering [of news] that goes on. Television is a collaborative medium. At any level it's a collaborative medium, and everything goes through several hands. Whether it's the piece that every reporter does, [it] goes through the hands of an editor or director or what have you . . . the decision making goes through several hands. So, every day I'm concerned not because we're doing it wrong—I'm concerned that we might do it wrong when that filtering comes in.[11]

Most television reporters can relate to stories of how show producers, on slow news days, lament that they have so much time to fill. Those producers often will settle for stories of a lesser importance, knowing that the story can be "turned" and completed in time to make the show deadline. Or television producers will often settle for a shorter blurb of a story, called a v/o (voice-over) or a sound-bite, than a full, balanced video package. And sometimes what starts out as a potentially good story fizzles away. Assignment editor Kelly Barnicle notes,

> When you're sitting here on the assignment desk, you always check it out because it could be anything. It could be really wrong or it could be fact-based. So for us—you have to check it out. And you just have to keep calling and checking and checking. By the time it gets to the producers, sometimes it's developed into a story—sometimes not. So, we check on a lot of things that never go anywhere. We're always checking with police, checking with fire [departments], checking with neighbors to see what's going on. And if we have a crew we'll send them by, sometimes, because they can tell us—it just depends on the circumstances. Quite often, it falls off the radar before you can even see what happened. So we have to worry about everything.[12]

In his *Mass Communication Theory*, Denis McQuail argued that a number of studies have pointed to a central truth: news is predictable and stable over time. Such a finding suggests that standard routines and cycles are at work in the newsgathering process . . . often tied to the essential standardized routines and cycles of organizations.[13] Many news operations have daily meetings in the mornings and afternoons during which the stories of the day are discussed and reporters are given their assignments to cover "selected" stories.

To keep news predictable and stable, news organizations have strategies to deal with uncertainty. Paul M. Hirsch, professor of strategy and organizations at Northwestern's Kellogg School of Management, argues that organizations seek ways to handle uncertainty to make their work more manageable.[14] One Chicago television station requires reporters to bring their "own" story ideas to daily meetings. The strategy ensures that a greater variety of news will be covered, allowing the station to praise itself, in on-air promos, for its "original reporting."[15]

CATEGORIES AND TYPES OF STORIES

A journalistic organization like a television newsroom looks for a blend of "hard news" and "soft news," of enterprising stories and human interest stories. Murders, violent crimes, and natural disasters make up the majority of breaking news. Still, efforts are made to offer the audience a variety of stories, knowing that different stories appeal to different people. Jennifer Lyons comments, "We are watching Google Analytics all the time so I know what stories are popping on the website and throughout the day. This can also help us make a decision on what stories we do."[16]

Often, television stations will interrupt programming with "banners" or headlines proclaiming, "Breaking News" or "Developing Story." These attempts to alert the viewer to an impending important story are often deceptive means to "grab" audience members by making them think the station they are viewing is better than its competition at covering news. (Many times, in reality, the banners sometimes precede "warmed-over" stories that are hours old and can be seen on television stations across the city. Continued use of these attention-grabbing "boy-who-cried-wolf" devices ends up being counterproductive because viewers eventually become numb to the blaring pronouncements. Thus, when a real tragedy occurs the audience may not immediately distinguish between a legitimate big event and one that has been "hyped up.")

But while this book was being written, a general manager of a television station in Louisville, Kentucky, decided not to use the phrase "breaking news" on his station. Calling it a marketing ploy, he felt that overuse of the headline misled the public.[17]

On the other hand, "types of stories" instruct news workers on the ways to handle and write these stories. Journalists are able to characterize types of stories by offering typical examples. A murder report, for instance, could be used to "symbolize" what is meant by "hard news." If an event is deemed hard news, the story is typically written in an inverted pyramid style with the most important news at the top: who, what, when, where, and why. The information is arranged in descending order of importance. The most important material is placed at the beginning of the story, and, usually, less important material follows. Subsequent paragraphs clarify and support the lead.

A typical murder allows the reporter to efficiently employ the following journalistic elements needed to tell the story.

Timeliness is stressed in a hard news story. What is the latest event to happen and when did it occur? The drive-by shooting or street gang murder usually happens with such a loud racket that witnesses can pinpoint the time the crime happened. When multiple murders occur, a team of reporters may be dispatched to go live for the next newscast, adding to the feeling of immediacy.

On the contrary, if a story is typified as a "soft news" piece, both timeliness and the inverted pyramid style of writing are less important. Instead, a narrative style may be chosen that uses scenes, anecdotes, and dialogue to build to a high point. People are prominent in the story, and quite often they are responsible for the action. The story has a beginning, a middle, and an end. In addition, if a story is categorized as soft news, there is no rush to run the story on a busy news day.

But there are exceptions to this rule. In the Deborah Evans story, I gave all the pertinent information at the beginning of my story. But because of the magnitude of the murder, I was given additional time to give my report. I broke from traditional, formal reporting and used my army background as a focal point to help clarify the details of the story. Judging by the reaction, the audience really appreciated my storytelling.

Murders are by nature dramatic. The murders that are chosen for coverage, the words used to describe them, and the ways in which these events are reported all affect the audience's interpretation of the information. Dr. Carl Bell, a psychiatrist who treats violent teens in his Chicago-based practice, thinks this heavy reliance on murder stories is dishonest to viewers. Bell, whom I met over thirty years ago, has published more than five hundred articles on mental health and is the author of *The Sanity of Survival.* He states,

> So, the media is in business to sell airtime or print. And so they're looking for hooks. And often those hooks are things that speak to people's fight, flight, or freeze system in the brain—the amygdala. And so violence leads, blood leads, tragic stories lead—heart-tugging stories lead, but it distorts the public's perspective of what's really going on. It turns out that homicides are down 50 percent all over the entire United States, but you'd never know that until you read it in the news.[18]

Routines: Customary practices are used to help organizations manage their workloads. The routine of "beats" (specific areas or levels of government where a reporter specializes—crime, education, finance, etc.) are like a news reservoir in which reporters visit established sites and talk with officials deemed of "obvious" interest to the audience: police officials, government agencies, major business leaders, etc. Routines help the news organization deal with the uncertainty of gathering news. And in many major cities like Chicago, on a slow news day, producers will often say, "Just wait, something will break." That makes it easy to produce the news product, even on slow days when very little is going on. Also on those sluggish days, reporters are sometimes given the routines of "beat checks," when daily calls are made to sources to determine if anything of news value has occurred.[19]

Crime reporters who cover a beat can generally come up with a good story to take up space or time in a news program or newspaper. General assignment reporters, on the other hand, are given stories to cover by their editors or the assignment desk. By contrast on busy news days, editors must decide among the choices of stories to cover.

Objectivity in murder cases is seldom needed by reporters. You would be hard-pressed to find instances when there was a need to justify a murder. Seasoned reporters are trained to solicit responses to most occurrences from two opposing sides. They are also trained to heavily quote from those sources, carefully placing those citations within quotation marks or using sound bites from video. The objective journalist refrains from taking any side as story narrator, lest the reporter offends the audience.

This perspective embodies the notion of "news construction." It suggests that news audiences come to learn about the world by what the media offers audiences and that the media tells the audiences about the world based on the organizational concerns of the media.

Economics: Media economists such as Bruce M. Owen stress that news is principally dependent on cost and revenue constraints. This is evident almost yearly when news directors go "over budget" because of some unforeseen event and have to cut back on overtime, travel to stories, and the use of helicopters.[20]

Owen contends that news organizations must work to maximize audiences because of the advertising-supported nature of news in the United States. Similarly, Dan Berkowitz and Douglas W. Beach argue, "Because media organizations are profit-making enterprises, journalists must learn to select and gather news that will draw a large audience."[21] But in a practical sense, journalists I have known and spoken with over a forty-five-year career seldom, if ever, think about the economics of gathering the news. Retired news director Greg Caputo pictures his viewers but not so much how and where they spend their advertising dollars:

> I've always thought of the audience, even as a news director, and all the things I just said about [news] being a business. I've been very

lucky that I've been able to . . . treat it with the sort of egalitarian attitude that I brought into it thirty years ago. So, I feel pretty lucky in that regard. I've worked for people who have allowed me that luxury.[22]

Yet, as producers follow the exact and precise feedback given by Internet websites, news organizations are discovering that traditional values of reporting and covering news have changed. As critical viewership has crashed over the decades, viewers have left traditional broadcast, over-the-air television, in favor of "on demand" previously recorded programming, cable, Internet television, and mobile programming. Now, the web audience is more interactive with the station, and that has changed views about presenting news to the public. Jennifer Lyons calls it a new day. "A couple of years ago," Lyons says, "we made the decision—when the website was getting big—that we were no longer a TV station, [but] we were a content provider."[23]

AUDIENCE IMAGE

Today, journalists know from Internet metrics exactly who is watching and when. Unlike decades ago when all you knew was that "a lot of people were watching the same program at the same time," that is not the case today. Yet there has not been very much written concerning just *how* the audience factors into the news.[24] Assignment editors defend their decisions by arguing identical perceptions. The editors want to give the audience something that will cause them to tune in day after day, night after night. And murders in the same neighborhoods, time after time, are not as spectacular as murders in a new or unusual area—the drive-by murder eventually loses its "wow effect." Kelly Barnicle says,

If it's weekend shootings and . . . if you're shot in the arm—if you're shot in the leg, you're definitely not going to get attention [by the assignment desk] because there's too many others to look into. If you're twenty-five years old as opposed to a twelve-year-old, you're not going to get the attention that the twelve-year-old is going to get. And some of the stories just turn out to be, just, that it was . . . gang related—not to say that we don't cover any gang shootings—but, as we're learning, the more that you ignore finding out that all of these innocent people are caught in the crossfire . . . that's why it's getting so much attention.[25]

News workers realize that a heterogeneous audience is watching, with a multitude of interests to which news organizations must appeal. Data from Internet websites seems to back up that contention.

On an institutional level, Phyllis Kaniss, in her book *Making Local News*, asks the question, "Why do crimes and accidents earn more news coverage than development and policy issues affecting thousands of people?"[26] Psychiatrist Carl Bell explains why:

We are so stuck on a deficit model of demonizing—because we have in our brains a voyeuristic, perverse wish to see the nasty, and the bloody, and the dirty, and the, you know, unmentionable. When people are driving down the highway, past a car accident, and everybody slows down, they want to see the blood and the disaster.[27]

Kaniss also criticizes the news media's undue focus on city events and assumes that the "actual" audience has a preference and a need for something different: news carefully gathered from suburban areas as well.[28] When television stations mostly report violent crimes from within the inner city and less from suburban areas, a misconception develops. Viewers begin to think of the urban area as less safe—and the residents who live there as being more violent—concluding that the suburbs are much safer. But, in reality, violent crime does indeed break out everywhere. Dr. Bell says,

[T]here is a huge problem in America and a huge tension between public health and the media. So, if you look at public health statistics and epidemiology—what we've learned about crime—black males and white males around eighteen perpetrate pretty much the exact same levels of violence . . . especially when viewed and controlled for socioeconomic [factors]—a poor white male has the same homicides as a poor black male; they are just disproportionately [more] poor black males.[29]

On an individual level, a variety of mass communications researchers argue that journalists don't really know their audiences. That might have been the case a decade or two ago, but today, through Internet and social media platforms, journalists are getting a clearer picture of their audience profile. Former executive producers like Sandy Pudar are constantly checking their web pages to learn what's trending and what viewers think about the shows. "It comes down to your gut in the morning," Pudar explains. "I know there are times when I stop and think, 'What's my fifty-four-year-old mother think about this?' And it's just not enough time in the day to consider all that."[30]

More and more, journalists do have some working sense of their audience, whether accurate or not. In David M. White's "Gatekeeper" study, the newspaper editor he studied offered this description of his audience: "Our readers are looked upon as people with average intelligence and with a variety of interests and abilities. I see them as human and with some common interests. I believe they are all entitled to news that pleases them and news that informs them."[31]

WGN-TV editor Pat Curry summed up audience perception about gangbangers this way: "People at home are not interested in hearing about bad guy versus bad guy—they just don't care."[32]

And neither do assignment editors and producers, according to the survey they completed in chapter four. By a wide margin, journalists favored covering a group of black teens who were killed while walking to school over a group of black teens who were murdered while shooting dice.

These insights help gatekeepers decide which stories they think will appeal to viewers. You wouldn't expect producers to—over and over—put on stories that they knew offended and turned off their audience. While researchers may argue that perceptions of the audience are vague and unclear at the level of the individual journalist, those who study journalistic construction from the organizational level of analysis see that notions of the audience are embedded within organizational routines and practices. News organizations often employ "special stories" that news directors think will be audience draws (e.g., "Medical Watch," "Action News on Your Side," and "Consumer Interest Investigators").

As such, the audience is used by journalists to convince their editors and producers of a story's merit and also used by organizations to sell to advertisers. And on rare occasions reporters will come up with an idea to use a "sponsored" segment in the broadcast to pitch an idea for a story that will fit well within that news block. From this perspective, working images of the audience are shaped to meet organizational needs. Those same audience images become embedded in organizational practice.

This manner of thinking coincides with Greg Caputo's revelation that his anchorman coworker was correct when the anchorman said, "News is what I say it is." This dogmatic way of thinking *is* correct. Viewers only watch one television station at a time. They may switch back and forth more often in recent years than they did before the invention of the remote control, but for the most part viewers are habitual and watch the same news anchor team day after day.[33]

But editors and producers often concern themselves with petty, nonessential details like the following: Which was the first station to report a story? Who had a key interview with a local authority? Which station was the first to broadcast the first photo of some star's baby? Remember, viewers are watching only one station at a time, and when they saw any of those elements, it is of no consequence to them because they were not watching the other station to notice that something different was on the air. That is the honest reality of what the audience sees. But, producers and news directors worry so much about the competitive aspect of reporting the news that often the audience is shortchanged.

Many times a well-produced, good story may run on a morning or noon program and be killed before it can air on the 5:00 p.m. show. Producers fear that the story is *stale* and *old*. What they forget is that viewers who were working day shifts never saw the story the first two times it aired. So, they will miss out entirely on seeing a compelling story because the producer was more interested in filling the show with fresh, new material. There is nothing wrong with being conscientious and wanting to work with new material, but savvy producers will run the good story on the later newscast, anyway. They know that if the story is absorbing, viewers will watch it over and over again because it is worth it. That way everyone gets to see the worthwhile story—in place of something that was frivolous and just taking up airtime.

Indeed the modern thrust of many news organizations seems to be a desire to grab their audiences and cater to them. In this sense, the audience is again treated as aggregate numbers or as a market to be captured. Many times when a major murder story has occurred, producers and editors will work to find associated stories that other reporters can cover and that follow the original case. This "team coverage" allows stations to expand on what is considered to be a major news event and also "personalize" the story by interviewing neighbors or friends of the victim or teachers—anyone who can give extra flavor or depth to the story.

Murders, especially of prominent individuals, as in the O. J. Simpson case, are played on news programs frequently. It could be argued that given the decline in newspaper readership and network viewership figures in the past few years, the current organizational perspective of the audience typically poses the audience as a market to be captured, to meet the goals of the news organization. That view of "audience as market" serving the news industry is also evidenced at the institutional level of analysis.

Modern expectations about the technology available to news practitioners also convey assumptions about the news production process, as it relates to murder coverage, and the way in which the audience retrieves the news. One common portrayal of the news audience, from those who focus on the changing technological picture of news production, is the audience as "techno-nerds" with a host of technological tools at their disposal to help them design the news for themselves. Web producer Elyse Russo explains that model:

> I try to do a mix. . . . I look at and use something called Google Analytics, and it's going to show me in real time what people are looking at and clicking on, and if something is doing well and being seen on the page. But, it's not going to be the only thing that I take into account.[34]

GUT FEELINGS TELL JOURNALISTS WHAT'S NEWS AND WHAT ISN'T

If there is one level of operational conflict in a newsroom that always seems primed for heated discussion, it is between the assignment desk and reporters. Reporters are quick to complain that "this is a crappy story" when given an assignment that might be unpopular. Assignment editors are hasty to counter that "I, too, know what news is. I've been doing this for a long time." The problem arises when both news workers rely on their gut instincts to guide them in selecting a story to be covered or not.

Both journalists see the same story from different perspectives. Reporters judge the story on the merits of how the finished story will look on the air and what it will take to tell the story. Sometimes, complex stories require a certain amount of research and analysis. The reporters also think about opposing sides of the issue and how difficult or easy it will be to track down those elements and still make a deadline. Chris Neale has been working the assignment desk for over twenty years. He can recognize a good news story right away—but he still has to consider many different parameters before he assigns a crew to the story. "It is kind of a gut feeling," Neale says, "and it's time and space—what time of day did this happen? A shooting in broad daylight may get our attention a little more than something that happened at two o'clock in the morning."[35]

But, I have observed heated confrontations among members of the assignment desk team as the tensions of the day and the constant stresses of the job come to a boil. Chris adds,

> And you're under constant deadline pressure—constant, unending deadline pressure . . . and if the story doesn't get on its way back to the station—either physically back or with a Dejero box [a cell phone–like platform for sending broadcast signals live or back to the newsroom] or microwave or satellite or any of these other technical things—it's not really news to us. It's not until the public gets it—way back here in the news.[36]

The genius of "assembly-line" production is to economically produce numerous identical products, but the goal of media arts production is to cheaply produce marginally different products, each of which, it is hoped, will be more attractive to prospective customers. The means of doing this is to produce many more items at each stage of the production process than will be accepted at, and successfully passed through, the next stage. Having newscasts that run consecutively allows for the "replay" of certain stories with little or no changes to the copy, and the same video can be used as well. Another hour of broadcast time has been filled and paid for by sponsors—yet very little expense in capital was incurred by the television or radio station.

In order to help filter out the excessive amount of potential stories waiting to be covered, news gatekeepers sort through the items that are produced each day and choose the appropriate pieces for broadcast. This is not so much the case in today's economically driven newsrooms. News directors must constantly choose whether to allow for such expensive items as overtime or the use of a news helicopter (during breaking news coverage), whether to send crews to cover out-of-town assignments, and whether to cut back on video shot by stringers (freelance camerapeople).

CRAFT AND ENTREPRENEURSHIP. This structure casts the reporter as a skilled crafts worker and focuses on the coordination of the various crafts worker's tasks within an organization. (Today, as unions have given up precious jurisdictions, many jobs within news organizations have become consolidated.) When consumer tastes are changing rapidly or are difficult to judge, one person is often put in charge of overseeing the efforts of artisans from the beginning to the end of the production process. In the news organization, such a task is typically assigned to the executive producer or news director. These individuals also become the filterers who may decide how the story is going to be played once it is back in the newsroom.

Will the murder receive top-story treatment or be "floated" and allowed to sit on the side, only to be used if extra time becomes available?

THE PRODUCT IMAGE. This implies that a successful media product will usually be fashioned in such a way as to resemble past successes. The ultimate goal is to please decision makers at the next level in the chain of command. Specifically, a focus on product image is flexible enough so that practitioners can mold their product to be like the most successful products of the recent past. In news theory, this implies that reporters will likely fashion their stories to resemble the structure of stories that were last considered a "standout" story by their editors. If a reporter won an Emmy for the way a murder story was covered, in all likelihood, the reporter would want to go about his or her reporting duties in the same manner for the next murder, as was done with the award winner.

The news producer will seek to organize newscasts in the same way that newscasts are traditionally organized. Graphics and story construction will likely follow successful styles. In strongly competitive markets a new station general manager—coming from a smaller market and bringing along a "small-town" mentality—may instruct his or her promo department to begin using blaring headlines and breaking news banners on a willy-nilly basis, until the manager learns that the accepted styles of a particular city frown on that type of presentation. Then, the new manager will settle down into a more conventional presentation.

If one assumes that the story or newscast is the key concern for the news worker, one must also consider the values inherent in that "product image." Once those values are delineated it is possible to discover how subtle audience imagery plays a part in the construction of news. At television stations where glaring images and breathless anchors are the style at that station, audience members will follow that station if they like that broadcast manner. Likewise on most public broadcast stations, a more "highbrow" means of constructing the news format is probable. PBS stations, for instance, are aware of the college-educated demographic of their audience, not fearing to use a lot of twelve-letter words in their stories.[37]

At WGN-TV, the station learned years ago that their tag line, "Chicago's Very Own," was a popular and effective means for grabbing viewers when local events merited covering.[38] In fact, the line was so useful in drawing in viewers that the slogan became a constant part of the station marketing plan.

For decades, textbooks on reporting have discussed the classic elements of news. Criteria most often considered to determine news-worthiness include the following:

PRODUCER DECISIONS ON NEWSWORTHINESS. Television producers and editors meet daily to decide which murder stories will be covered. Their decisions determine which slayings viewers will come to know as news. A report of a current event counts as news and is newsworthy by virtue of its being broadcast—the "News Is What I Say It Is" model.

As producers and editors grapple with the decision of which murders to cover and how, the question of "significance" often arises. But significance is "relative" to the opinions of each viewer.

If two major events happened simultaneously, say, the terrible murder of Deborah Evans and the destruction of the *Mona Lisa* in Paris, significance would differ greatly among the people affected by the events. To Parisians living in Paris, the desecration of their prized masterpiece would be unparalleled and they would never even hear about Evans. But to Evans's neighbors, her death would be the greater story.

In each case, local producers in Paris or Chicago would have no trouble deciding which story would be their lead or top story.

Of course there are many other elements that will also affect the decisions on which murders to cover and which to ignore:

- **Proximity.** Is the story relevant to local viewers?
- **Conflict.** Is the issue developing, has it been resolved, or does anybody care?
- **Eminence or prominence.** Are noteworthy people involved? If so, that makes the story more important.
- **Consequence or impact.** What effect will the story have on readers?
- **Human interest.** Even though it might not be an earth-shattering event, does it contain unique, interesting elements?

As newsroom leaders struggle to decide which stories to include, they use these elements so often that they become part of the "gut feelings" that journalists rely on to help them make split-second decisions. And most of the time they are correct.

Chapter Three

THE HISTORY OF THE CHANGING BROADCAST FORMAT

Before we go further into what is happening in journalism today, and how murder cases are considered, it might be significant to set the stage for how broadcast news developed over the last sixty years and how murder cases were covered. Some interesting patterns have emerged just within my lifetime. And, as I reflect on the status of television news today, I can't help but remember how the electronic manner of informing the public began.

The paradigm for electronically disseminating news information about murders, to the public, has continued to evolve over the years. But the most noteworthy discovery is that the model has halved itself with each change.

Every time a major shift in the manner of reporting news has occurred, the earlier method only lasted half as long as the preceding system it replaced, and that lasted only half as long as the one that came before it. I have witnessed these changes and have been intimately involved with each paradigm shift.

Much of what general assignment reporters cover when a murder has been committed has to do with either the crime itself, the investigation, or, in a few cases, the suspects who are caught, prosecuted, convicted, and sentenced to prison. So it is safe to say that over half of my professional forty-five-year journalistic career has been about telling news stories dealing with crime in general and murders in particular.

79

MURDER IN THE NEWS

My earliest childhood memories are of people telling me stories. My mother and two of her five sisters always read to me when I was a toddler, while my father was away during World War ll. And once he returned from overseas when the war ended, I would be enchanted listening to his imaginary battle stories—yarns my dad would spin about fighting the Germans single-handedly while protecting his frightened friend, Harry.

So, it's not surprising to me that my adult life has been in the pursuit of storytelling—reporting news and feature stories and later handling documentary production in my own company, Video Family Biographies. All of it involves telling stories.

I have often conjectured that storytelling goes back to the earliest form of communication. Once again I think of Og, the primitive caveman, who after being killed was mourned for who knows how long—because he was the fire keeper and his life was instrumental to the well-being of the clan. Og would have, no doubt, been prominent in the eyes of his peers and would have held a special place on the social-economic ladder of his group.

Growing up, I had no idea that my professional life would entail writing and that journalism would consume the second half of my life. The thought that I would be at thousands of murder scenes over the course of my adult life would have been abhorrent to me.

I firmly believe that part of my ability to rely on my imagination comes from the days of radio. In the 1940s, during the so-called "golden days" of radio, I was a preschooler who would be glued to the front of our console Zenith radio, sitting as closely to it as possible—as if being next to the speaker made me nearer to Superman, Sergeant Preston of the Yukon, or the Shadow. Murders were seldom the main theme of the program, but there was still a clear line between the bad guys and good guys. And very few black people were on radio; the ones who were held menial jobs. They spoke poor English, broke verbs, and were portrayed in a negative manner. Even programs where there were colored or Negro (as African Americans were called in those days) characters, they were maids or chauffeurs—not businesspeople or teachers or reporters or doctors or scientists.

Radio shows were so compelling, due to their creative sound effects people, that I could visualize what was taking place during the program. When Sergeant Preston of the Yukon—over the howling scream of freezing, whistling winds—shouted, "On King, on you Huskies," I could visualize him standing at the rear of his dogsled, whip in hand, urging his splendid team of yelping dogs to strain at their harnesses as they chased a villain or raced at blazing speed from one snow-covered location to another. I could imagine Superman streaking through the skies at an insane velocity—because, after all, he was faster than a speeding bullet.

Radio, in the forties, was a wonderful magic flying carpet that could transport you anywhere in a vivid, lifelike manner. Your only restriction was your imagination. I can remember my disappointment when I saw my first photo of the Lone Ranger. He and Tonto were nothing like I had imagined them to be.

I remember the only program that was dedicated to defining what life was like in Negro homes: *Amos 'n' Andy*, a comedy that portrayed black people to be ignorant, childish, and lacking any defining social graces.

These early disparaging ways in which African Americans were depicted laid the groundwork for how television in the early days would portray a whole race of people. These negative stereotypes would become ingrained in the psyche of American thinking and would form the foundation for bolstering and supporting segregation, Jim Crow, and other forms of racial inequality.

Not just African Americans were the subjects of this sordid treatment by mainstream media. In cowboy movies, Native Americans were seldom permitted to do more than grunt. They were called savages and killed by the thousands (on film and in real life). Chinese

Americans rarely did more than work in kitchens or on the railroads and were made into sad caricatures who mumbled in unintelligible voices. Mexicans and other Latin movie characters were also ridiculed and mocked because of their accents and dress.

This was the continuation of the unspoken campaign by the media to carry on the subjugation of black Americans and other people of color. Ad agencies also participated in this atrocious dehumanization of a whole race by using demeaning, vicious caricatures of colored people on their products. Most of the time, if black people weren't depicted in marketing campaigns in a disparaging manner, they were just left out altogether.

But while Sergeant Preston fought imaginary criminals on radio, real crime statistics were increasing in large cities like New York and Chicago. According to the Chicago Crime Scenes Project, Chicago is a perfect city to examine in this book:

> [B]etween 1870 and 1920, Chicago's crime rate grew at an essentially steady pace, reaching a peak of ten per 100,000 in 1919. During this period, Chicago was growing in population and density. High population density is typically associated with greater crime rates for several reasons. First, in small towns, every face is familiar, but in large cities, criminals are less likely to be recognized by witnesses. Realizing a lower likelihood of being caught, criminals commit more crimes. Second, crime pays better in cities, because there are more people to rob—there's no point in becoming a robber in the first place if you can't hit lots of targets. Finally, and especially relevant to Chicago during this period, big cities attract large communities of poor immigrants with few prospects for legal employment. Being a criminal, on the other hand, is a profession that is open to all.[1]

But like most American youngsters during the 1940s and 1950s, I had no notions of criminality, other than what I saw in the movies.

THE HISTORY OF THE CHANGING BROADCAST FORMAT

The doors to our Nashville, Tennessee, home were seldom locked. Throughout my childhood, I never heard a gunshot. My parents (my father was a dentist and my mother a college professor) and everyone I knew were the opposite of the almost subhuman characters illustrated in newspapers or seen in magazines. So, like most black kids of that era, I grew up constantly feeling resentment and bitterness because the media was frequently offending me by the way my race was being wrongly defined. And decades later, as a television reporter, I would find myself working behind the "media curtain" that determines what goes out to the public for consumption.

When I was in the first or second grade, my good friend Medrid Dennis told me that his father had just bought something called a television. He described the device as being a big box containing a little screen, like a radio with movies inside. I couldn't wait to see this unbelievable contrivance.

Med told me to come by his house around 5:00 p.m., when the programs would begin coming on. I was there at 4:00. We sat and watched the tiny twelve-inch screen, looking at the test pattern for an hour, mesmerized by the light and the black-and-white image coming out of the console. Then, when the first program came on—a crudely produced cowboy show called *Western Corral*—I was enthralled. What was this enchanting device that brought picture stories right into your home?

Med's father told us that television would eventually kill radio— that no one would want to *listen* to programs when they could *see* what was going on at the same time. I remember thinking how upsetting it would be if radio did go away. I worried about that for a long time. If radio disappeared, what would happen to all of my friends— Superman, the Lone Ranger, Sergeant Preston, and all the rest? This television thing was unsettling to me yet thrilling at the same time.

Day after day, I would stop by Med's house to watch television. And even though television was still in its infancy and was pretty much glorified radio—radio that you could see—it was nonetheless trans-forming. Finally, my father bought a television, bringing the magic of movies and variety shows right into the living room of our house.

Even as a child, I knew that television was greater than radio—radio, the friend that had fed my inextinguishable imagination. Radio, my source of hours of pleasure, was now inferior. A new broadcast medium now owned the airwaves. The cyclopic box with its piercing beam of information was mesmerizing.

But soon, I was seeing the same monstrous depictions that had haunted me as a child when I looked at Aunt Jemima syrup, or Uncle Ben's rice (both of which have had their logo images of black people softened over the years), or saw *Amos 'n' Andy*, now on the screen, or the thousands of other negative images that Madison Avenue thrust upon the public. (Search online for Aunt Jemima and see some of the denigrating images Quaker Oats used over the years.)

There were no news programs during those early days of televi-sion. News came from radio. As a boy growing up in both Atlanta and Nashville, I never heard of a murder or knew of anyone who had been shot. The first time I ever saw a murder victim or knew about a violent death was in *Jet* magazine, the lynching of Emmett Louis Till. Till was an African American boy who was murdered in Mississippi at the age of fourteen after reportedly whistling (flirting) at a white woman. *Jet* published a horrifying photo of Till's badly beaten and unrecognizable body. His mother released the photo because she wanted the world to see what had been done to her child. For many weeks I couldn't sleep at night after seeing that photo.

Up to that point in history, the only place to see what was going on in the world was the cinema. Fox newsreels were originally seen prior to feature films in movie theaters around the world, starting in 1919 with the silent Fox news service. Fox Movietone was estab-lished in 1926, and the first Movietone newsreels were exhibited January 21, 1927, at the Sam Harris Theater in New York City and ending in 1963 shortly before the assassination of President John F. Kennedy.[2] A favorite subject of the early newsreels was aviation. One of the most significant events of the twentieth century was photographed on May 20, 1927, when a Movietone camera crew filmed Charles Lindbergh taking off from Roosevelt Field on his celebrated transatlantic flight from New York to Paris. The raw film negative was rushed back from Long Island to be processed or developed. Later, a print was projected for euphoric audiences at the Roxy Theatre in Manhattan—the same evening of that very day—inspiring Fox to create Movietone News.

This process of shooting film at a big event or news scene and getting it out to the public would not change for the next fifty years. This would be the way audiences would *see* faraway news events. But black people wouldn't be in many of the newsreels.

The cameras in the 1920s and 1930s were huge, heavy contraptions with large Mickey Mouse–ear film magazines attached on the top of the camera. The cameras were mounted on heavy, wooden tripods. And for mobility, the camera crews could stand in the back of a station wagon that had the top cut out—almost like a pickup truck except it was a car. They also carried smaller Bell & Howell handheld cameras that shot silent film.

The newsreels established a format that network news broadcasts follow to this day (local stations usually lead off with a big local story). World events generally led off the program, followed by stories of national interest. A fashion or entertainment piece would round out the show before ending with the sports segment. Between 1919 and 1963 Fox Movietone produced 4,578 biweekly newsreels.[3]

My childhood friends and I—during the late forties and early fifties—went to the movie theater every weekend. Tickets were a quarter, and for another quarter you could buy a hot dog and a soda pop. A box of popcorn was a dime. And you would get to see a double feature plus a cartoon. We never called ahead—we just showed up, usually in the middle of the movie. You would just stay to see the movie back around to the point where someone in the group would say, "I think this is where we came in." Then we would leave.

The fifteen-minute Movietone reel with news and features was my favorite. You could see exotic, faraway places and learn what was happening across the globe. The only black people you ever saw were entertainers like Sammy Davis Jr. and the leaders of big jazz bands, like Duke Ellington and Count Basie or singers like Ella Fitzgerald or Lena Horne.

Two things happened that increased the amount of news that was fed to audiences: cameras became smaller and war broke out. World War II was the first time actual news reporters were used to tell stories. Before then, beginning in the late 1920s, early radio news was usually nothing more than a dramatized documentary of events. There were no live recordings, and limited technology made it hard to produce. News events were dramatized as producers thought this approach would have a more effective impact.[4]

An early form of this approach was the radio program *March of Time,* where a narrator would dramatize news stories. Roy Larsen, who'd go on to become president of Time Inc., was the producer.[5] Years later, after World War II, in 1945, the program *Unshackled* was broadcast, in its first incarnation, from the Pacific Garden Mission in Chicago.[6] The mission is a shelter for homeless men and women. The radio program has a live audience composed of the clients who flock to the shelter on frigid nights during the brutal Chicago winters and others who came to hear the weekly message of redemption and salvation.

Today, a little over seventy years since it began, *Unshackled* is still broadcast live with actors standing before microphones—reading from scripts—while a sound effects engineer, working with all kinds of contraptions, makes sounds mimicking doors opening and closing, produces "real-sounding" footsteps of characters and sounds of glasses filled with ice cubes that clink, while distant train whistles scream in the distance. I have witnessed these performances many times and to do so is to travel back in time to observe the medium of radio as it was during the so-called "golden days."

Radio listeners also received their news this way at the time. I remember watching my parents and grandparents as they gathered around the huge console Zenith radio, the size of a hotel room minibar. In the early 1940s, this was where everyone listened intently to reports from the war. The news copy was written in a more descriptive manner—suitable for radio. I remember being told by an Associated Press radio editor, named Al Green, that radio news copy was different from television scripts because of the need to assist the listener with descriptions that evoked mental images, not needed when watching television. Radio news was slowly becoming the kind of newscast that is well known today.[7]

In June 1970, I was back in Nashville, Tennessee. My family had moved to Atlanta, Georgia, from Nashville when I was twelve years old, and I continued to grow up in Atlanta. But after my lackluster college days at Morehouse College were interrupted by the Vietnam War, I returned to Nashville to finish college at Fisk University after my army days were over.

In need of a job, in the summer of 1970 I had heard that a television station was looking to hire its first people of color for on-air work. So I went to the station, WSM Television—an NBC affiliate—and applied. After a few times of being called back for more interviews and meetings, I was hired.

I can remember how thrilled I was to actually walk into the studio from where I had, twenty-five years before, seen my first television program broadcast—*Western Corral*. Now, the station had another claim to fame: it was the station that owned the Grand Ole Opry, the Valhalla of country music.

I was hired as a booth announcer in June 1970. During this time television stations had announcers who read commercials "live" from a broadcast booth every half hour, during station breaks.

I had been hired as the first black on-air personality at WSM Television. I was working for a television station, but it was as if I was on radio. You could hear me yet not see me. But soon, I was beginning to learn the business. I began appearing on a morning television country music program. I taught myself how to draw my weather maps based on data and information from the National Weather Service. I was a TV weatherman in the mornings and a newsreader for the rest of the day.

Working in a small- to medium-sized market like Nashville was like going to graduate school. I learned so much about television production and television news. I struck up a friendship with the radio news director, a crusty ex-AP (Associated Press) editor named Al Green. Al would give me wire copy to rewrite. I would work on it and give him back the copy, which he would redline and scratch through as if I were a third grader turning in bad homework. I worked with Al for about six months until I learned how to write copy that he approved of—stories that would make him smile.

As the only black person on the air at my station, I began covering news around Nashville. (Oprah Winfrey later began working for Channel 5 in Nashville just before I left town to move to Chicago.) Up until that time black people were rarely seen on television. News stories also seldom covered events in black neighborhoods or showed blacks in a flattering light. Even though there were two prominent black colleges, Fisk University and Tennessee State University, as well as a historic black medical school—Meharry Medical College—there still weren't many positive stories about black people that appeared on local television in Nashville. And when African Americans were on television, it was either singing or dancing or being depicted in a demeaning manner such as "shuffling," hat-holding, subservient housekeepers or maids (honorable jobs, nonetheless, but no lawyers or doctors or teachers or postal workers).

Psychiatrist Carl Bell points out that these stereotypes become a self-fulfilling prophecy. "The . . . issue is the perception that people of color have regarding the value of their lives," Bell explains. "[I]f all you see on the news are homeless people, you essentially sort of get the feeling—well, maybe that's okay; well, maybe we're not much [of] value."[8]

I stayed at WSM for three years, learning everything I could about the business. Then one day, in March 1973, I received a call from a man named Chuck Harrison. Chuck said he was the news director at WGN-TV in Chicago. He said he had seen me on the air when he was passing through Nashville and liked what he saw. He asked if I would be interested in working in Chicago. He offered to fly me to the city for an interview.

I remember the day I walked into WGN-TV for my interview. When I walked off the plane, Chuck was there to greet me. Back then, anyone could walk to the gate to meet a plane. On the way in to the station, he told me about my duties—I would be reporting the news.

In Nashville I hadn't worked very much as a reporter. I was the morning weatherman and the anchorman of the noon news. I had seldom reported from the scene of a story. When I did report from the scene, it was on election night or on a special story. So I was apprehensive about accepting the job.

Chuck told me about the wonderful history of WGN-TV and WGN Radio. I learned that the station had two helicopters for the number one radio program in the country—the Wally Phillips show. On the television side there was an equally iconic program called *Bozo's Circus*. The program was so popular, I was told, that when women became pregnant they would send in for tickets. And since the waiting list was seven years, the mothers-to-be would receive their tickets when their children were six or seven years old.

When Chuck and I pulled into the parking lot of the station, next to the heliport where two choppers were parked, I began to realize that working for this outfit was big-time.

Little did I know that a major paradigm shift was about to take place in news reporting, the first of many to come.

Chuck took me into the station to first meet the man, the general manager, who had built WGN-TV: the famous Ward Quall. Our meeting went well, and then Chuck took me to the other side of the building to show me the newsroom.

As we walked down the long hall leading to the newsroom, I could hear the shrill clatter of keys being hit on Underwood typewriters: dozens of typewriters in a smoky room full of people with their heads buried in their work. There were radio news writers working on the five- to ten-minute newscasts heard every thirty minutes. In another part of the room were television reporters and news writers and producers and assignment desk editors. This was a busy place.

After looking around the room, I realized that, like Nashville, I was the only black person in the room—there were no females either. Upon further examination, I did discover a black female secretary, Gloria Brown, who, I later learned, had just moved into the newsroom from the sales offices on the other side of the building (soon thereafter a black cameraman, Richard "Ike" Isaac, from a local film school, began working on an apprenticeship program).

It was March 1973, and I accepted the position at WGN-TV. My wife Sharon and our six-month-old daughter, Karen—who, thirty years later, would be my on-air competition when she anchored the weekend news for rival Channel 7 ABC News—joined me later that year in June. (Additionally, Karen's husband, Christian Farr, would be reporting for the NBC station in Chicago, making us a family with three members working on air in a major market.)

At the time, stations were making major efforts to hire minorities and women in local and national television. At WGN-TV, Merri Dee, Floyd Brown, and I were the new faces of color on the air. NBC hired Carole Simpson and Jim Tilmon, CBS hired Burleigh Hines and Harry Porterfield, and ABC brought in Bob Petty. But since there were no African Americans in gatekeeper positions—as assignment editors or producers—we still didn't cover a lot more uplifting stories from minority neighborhoods.

Covering news in Chicago was worlds apart from reporting stories in Nashville. A news team, or "crew," consisted of four people—a reporter, a cameraman, a sound technician, and a lighting man. We would all ride around in Ford Crown Victorias (because of the large trunk space), moving from story to story throughout the day.

We would stay connected to the assignment desk at the station via a two-way Motorola walkie-talkie radio the size and weight of a brick. Or if we needed to talk to someone at WGN-TV without the other stations listening in to our transmission—as we often did to see what each other was covering—you could pull over and use a pay phone (then found on every corner).

At breaking stories like multiple murders and large fires, the crews would be met at the scene by one of our two motorcycle couriers. The couriers would rush the news film to the lab to be processed. That would take about forty minutes for a four-hundred-foot roll of film. Then the couriers would grab the film and race to the television station so the film could be cut or edited. So, from the time an event occurred it couldn't make it on air for at least forty minutes to an hour or two. Aside from breaking stories like fires, murders, and other mayhem, most of the news consisted of organized press conferences held at the many hotels across the city.

Videotape made its debut in the late 1970s. The film crews had been reduced to "one-man bands" by then because the film cameras (CP-16 cameras) were smaller and used a type of film stock that contained a magnetic stripe on the side of the film for recording audio.[9]

But the new video tube cameras were big, bulky, and heavy. They were connected by an umbilical cord to an equally heavy audio box containing the video tape. So the crews went back to four men because you needed a soundman and also needed a lighting man.[10] The new video cameras also weren't very good in low light.

But because there was no film, there was no processing time. The couriers could meet you at the scene, grab the videotape, and race straight to the station. If necessary, the raw tape could be put on the air quickly. Greg Caputo was working as a writer/producer at WBBM-TV, a Chicago station owned by the CBS Television Network:

> During the seventies and early eighties the station started to adopt a lot of minicam reports in the field, and I think as that evolved, over the course of the late seventies, early eighties, into the mideighties, probably, it forced a new degree of discipline on the storyteller so that you had to be able to sustain and fully tell a story very quickly— it took away the time that reporters used to be able to spend, to form their thoughts and write the narrative to go with the story. When we had film processing, that was then fifteen, twenty, thirty, forty minutes—when the film was in the [developing] process— that the reporter couldn't do anything other than think about the story and put it together.
>
> Live television changed that. So that required a new degree of discipline on the reporters and also put into place an expectation on the part of the viewer that he would see events as they were happening.[11]

It was now 1976. I had been at WGN-TV for three years. Local news during those days consisted of a lot of fires, murders, press conferences, and features or human interest stories. We at WGN were still using film while all the other stations in Chicago had transitioned to videotape.

I applied to CBS Network News and was hired by a legendary newsman, Jack Smith. I began working under Jack in the Midwest Bureau out of the Chicago offices over the WBBM-TV Channel 2.

THE HISTORY OF THE CHANGING BROADCAST FORMAT

As a Midwest reporter working for the network, my stories were on *CBS Evening News with Walter Cronkite* or *CBS Morning News.* The Midwest Bureau covered stories of national import, mostly from Ohio, west to Colorado, and everything in between.

Working at the network was like going to postgraduate school. Now, there were four- or five-man crews. You also had a field producer who accompanied you on most stories, helping with the setup and doing a lot of the phone communication between Chicago and New York—when you were doing a farm story in a small town in Nebraska or a crime story in Detroit or a weather story in Duluth, Minnesota. It was exciting work. Murder stories were seldom covered at the network news level—that was left to the local stations to report (sensational cases, or multiple murders, were reported on the national level). But the travel was constant and seemingly never-ending.

In 1980, while I was still at CBS, WGN-TV began to expand its news coverage, becoming a "superstation." I saw this as an opportunity to stop traveling and to return to local news. I applied to WGN-TV and went back to my old home station. The electronic age was still in the midst of determining its direction. The paradigm had not fully completed its shift.

Television stations were using a format from Sony called Beta. But there was also another alternative called VHS that was competing with Sony. And there were even two types of electronic devices to support both formats: Beta recorders and VHS recorders. Video rental stores began popping up on every block to support a burgeoning industry of enjoy-at-home movies and programs. Usually in any industry, the better, higher-quality format wins out. But that was not to be the case in this war.

Television stations continued to support the Beta format because it was better, clearer, sharper, smaller, and more durable. VHS, on the other hand, was grainy, dull, and subject to glitches in the recorded product. And VHS was also cheaper. But that was not the deciding factor.

What determined the outcome of this battle was not triple-A-quality programming, but it was triple-X-rated video. The porn industry had standardized its library of videotapes on the VHS format. Men, primarily, who bought video recorders did so with the knowledge that their local video stores stocked movie material (also X-rated tapes) in mainly the VHS format. So VHS recorders quickly became the customary way for consumers to record and view video material.

Television coverage of news continued to evolve in the early 1980s. Caputo remembers that politics was a dominant feature of many newscasts:

> [T]his is just a view of a Chicago news guy. . . . In the rest of the country—in the newscasts of the seventies, for example—[there was] heavy emphasis on politics, heavy emphasis on social issues, heavy emphasis on those kinds of things that mattered, even into the eighties. And then there started to be a shift, and I think that some of those stories went by the boards or didn't get the same degree of emphasis at the lead of the show, or the development of the show, in favor of more visually stimulating [material], or at least something that evoked a visceral reaction.[12]

But the disparity with which minorities were covered remained constant, although in the midseventies more effort was made to cover issues in minority neighborhoods. (The local CBS station, WBBM, did open a bureau in Gary, Indiana—a predominately African American city—for a while, but that operation eventually closed.[13]) Stations began to experiment with microwave signals and soon learned that video could be sent from one location to another via microwave. Stations like WGN-TV were already sending their signals up to satellites. So receiving dishes were erected on tall buildings around cities.

To feed the signals to the dishes, stations began designing specially equipped vehicles called minicam trucks. Each truck contained a telescoping mast that, like a super long periscope, could be elongated to shoot a signal over the average house or building to hit the dish atop the John Hancock Building or Sears (now Willis) Tower.

Now breaking news could, for the first time, be broadcast live. A minicam truck driver could go to the scene, put up the mast, call the station, and talk to an engineer who would help the cameraperson orientate the sending dish atop the mast so the signal was hitting the receiving dish atop the Hancock Building. Once the signal was strongly hitting the receiving dish, you could go live.

By 1980, satellites, or "birds," as they were called, had been strung in a geosynchronous orbit around the earth. WGN became a so-called "superstation," broadcasting around this half of the earth via satellite, which brought in "snowbird" viewers from Florida and Arizona. The station expanded its news to an hour and also began to counterprogram, going on the air at 9:00 p.m. instead of 10:00 as the other local stations were doing.

Satellites hovering about 22,500 miles above the earth would relay most television programming to world viewers. Each "bird" was composed of a number of transponders, or independent receive-transmit units.

By the late eighties CNN had designed portable, freestanding satellite uplinks referred to as "flyaway units."[14] These mobile crews were introduced for electronic newsgathering (ENG) work. This meant that TV links could be quickly set up in remote locations—including foreign countries—to transmit news to viewers on the other side of the globe.

A flyaway satellite uplink, complete with a telephone link, was so compact that with only ten suitcases and a three-person crew, CNN reporters could fly anywhere around the globe—no matter how remote—and broadcast live from the scene. The shiny aluminum uplink dish collapsed like a flamenco dancer's fan and could be spread open to form a parabolic dish. Other cases contained batteries and chargers, camera and cables, a reflector, a tripod, a generator, and a couple of oscilloscopes. That's all it took to go live from the middle of the desert or the balcony of a hotel overlooking "shock and awe" as bombs fell on Baghdad.

This ability to quickly go live was good and bad: good in that news was getting to the audience more quickly, and bad in that the reporter had less time to gather information and check to make sure her report or story was accurate before putting it out over the air.

Reporters have always had deadlines, but historically those cutoff points were hours or days away. Now, a reporter had only moments before it was time to feed the beast. All of a sudden television stations had a new toy—the live shot. Greg Caputo says that in "the eighties and nineties, and certainly now, [the live shot] has become commonplace—the viewer expects it. . . . [T]hat's a big change in the way reporters and producers have to think about what they are doing—whether they have time to think about it."[15]

In a television-ratings-crazy business model, each station constantly tries to outdo the other to garner a larger audience. The more viewers you have, the more you can charge to sell advertising time. Over the years, this has caused some stations—not all—to come up with some of the dumbest, wackiest, ill-conceived ideas a desperate TV executive could think of.

Prior to the 1980s, television news had been a "loss leader" during the broadcast day. Stations didn't sell very much time during a newscast, just enough to help pay some of the salaries and buy new cameras and news vehicles. But news programming was, now, proving to be popular with viewers. Greg Caputo notes,

> The advent, as well, of some of the tabloid TV shows—*Current Affair* being the first one, *Inside Edition*, and some of the others that followed—also brought a viewer expectation that you could have that sort of show. A tabloid feel . . . I don't mean that in a negative way, in the sense of rumormongering or anything like that—tabloid at

its soul is something that evokes a visceral reaction . . . it makes you feel. Some of the best writing in the world makes you feel something—Hemingway makes you feel something. Nobody ever called him tabloid, but that's what tabloid is. It's an appeal to the feeling. The difference on tabloid TV is that it's a feeling, a feeling . . . only it doesn't necessarily require the analytical thought—and I think that was also a change brought about in TV news as it sort of grew up with its audience.[16]

During the 1970s and 1980s attitudes about covering events and stories dealing with black people continued to improve. In Chicago, the election of Harold Washington in 1983 did more to transform news coverage than any other event. Producers and assignment editors made concerted efforts to cover news in the "black community."

And in the late seventies and eighties, with swanky news sets—flashy news anchors and targeted efforts to draw in and increase ratings—news became a viable part of a station's bottom line. Caputo thinks the original mission of broadcast television changed:

I think a piece of the puzzle is the realization that television news can be a very profitable operation. And that brings with it its own series of demands. When something is looked at as a for-profit thing, obviously, TV stations have always been making money; that's nothing new. . . . [T]he evolutionary piece of this, in the period of time that I've been a news director, is that because you are now an important part of that profit center, you are looking at it as a business, not necessarily as a public service.[17]

General managers began adding additional newscasts and spending more money on glitzing up newscasts. Boosting ratings became such a driving force that desperate television bosses began hiring news consultants to help them increase their numbers.

MURDER IN THE NEWS

The leading consultant at the time was Frank Magid. Magid was known in particular for encouraging scores of local stations to adopt the "Action News" format, in which traditional news items were interspersed with a liberal dose of crime coverage, especially murders, and lighter entertainments like human interest stories.[18] He also inaugurated early-morning newscasts in many local markets.

To advise local news directors on ways to attract bigger audiences, Magid conducted extensive viewer surveys. The results could radically affect the look and sound of the program, from anchors' hair and attire to their on-air repartee. Magid was an early advocate of the convivial banter among anchors known as "happy talk."

But what concerns me the most about this sometimes reckless approach toward beating the competition was that *some* gullible news directors and general managers allowed Magid and his consultants to convince seasoned news journalists that writers should begin breaking all the rules of grammar. Magid's folks persuaded news directors to have their writers and reporters begin writing stories in the present tense, even for events that happened hours or days in the past.[19] Their specious rationale was that speaking in the present tense gave a sense of immediacy to the story. That's nonsense! Many anchors also began speaking in phrases—not complete sentences with verbs and other essential parts of speech. You probably sit at home and do a lot of, "What was that he said?"

But sooner or later, you're going to have to revert to the past tense in order to explain clearly when the events transpired. And at that time, I contend, you are confusing your audience. How often have you heard, "A fire breaks out in a high-rise"? No! It "broke" out in a high-rise because it happened this morning. But that is the baloney you have heard since the consultants—who were for the most part salesmen, not journalists—began advising broadcast executives. So the executives bought it. Newspapers never drank that bogus "Kool-Aid" and did not fall for the double-talk the consultants were spewing.

Most network reporters continue to use correct grammar except that many, improperly, use double subjects when speaking extemporaneously. For example, an anchor might say, "The president, he . . ." or "Today, Hillary Clinton, she . . ."

The videotape paradigm lasted for almost twenty-five years—half as long as film—as the main format for broadcasting news stories. By the middle to late nineties videotape was beginning to be phased out in favor of digital formats.

Entire newsrooms became digital; WGN-TV was one of them. For years writers had used five-page copy books—containing a carbon sheet between each page—on which to type stories. This was so everyone was "literally" on the same page. When the book was broken down, the pages went to the teleprompter, director, producer, and both anchors.

To make sure all the pages were in the proper places, the script piles would be stacked about thirty minutes prior to airtime. Blank filler pages containing only the "slug," or story title, were placed in spots where the finished scripts would eventually be placed. It was a laborious process, but it was done this way to make sure all the key people were reading the same page at the same time. Even so, pages would stick together or the prompter operator would sometimes mix up pages, meaning that anchors and directors would sometimes be on different stories . . . and that meant trouble.

So when newsrooms went digital, everything—the scripts, video, graphics, audio—would be digitized, and all of it went into a giant computer or server. Eventually, archived stories and all the historical information would be stored on the server as well.

In Chicago, on the streets, when crews were sent to a murder story to go live, the truck would pull up to the location, and the operator would raise the mast and begin aiming in the general direction of the Hancock Building or the Sears Tower. No longer was pinpoint accuracy necessary. With digital technology you could even bounce the signal off office buildings, making it ricochet like balls on a billiard table, until it hit the receiving dish. The minicam truck would also be where the story was edited, right on the laptop using one of the new editing programs like Final Cut Pro.

When reports of shootings would come into the newsroom, crews could be dispatched to the scene for a reporter to feed back a report. This was a quick way to lead off a segment in a newscast with an exciting story that could be opened with a breaking news banner. Often, breathless reporters standing in front of yellow crime scene tape would spend two minutes reporting the sad shooting of a child or an elderly resident. Sound bites from shocked neighbors and video of hysterical family members would comprise much of the story. Many times reporters would be goaded, by antsy producers, into going live before they even knew the names of the victims or had very much pertinent information to report. That didn't matter—going live was what counted. Father Michael Pfleger says this type of reporting is demeaning to the community because the victim is treated like a number—becoming a nameless corpse:

> We're determining the value of life. We're determining that some life is more valuable than others. I even get concerned when I see the media talk about, "Well he was a gangbanger—he was affiliated." Who determines that, number one? The media takes it from the police person saying that—or spokesperson saying that—but nobody investigates to see what does it mean? Does he have a record of gang affiliation or is he somehow invested in gang crimes or do they just put a sign on it?
>
> And when that becomes known in the media someone takes that and says because he or she is gang affiliated, that . . . that life is even less? We're supposed to say, "Well that's what they get," you know?[20]

Night after night and story after story viewers would be fed this steady diet of tragedy and inner-city violence; that format for news hasn't changed to this day. Psychiatrist Carl Bell sees this type of news coverage as blurring reality:

> When you look at violence that doesn't result in homicides—and is a felony level of violence—black males and white males do about the same. The reality, though, is that rarely does anyone black or white get caught during that level of violence. But, of course, homicide is easy to solve, to some extent. And it's harder to hide. And that's a problem. But the public has a distorted perception of who is violent.[21]

But with the new digital cameras being smaller and more sensitive to low light, and having a longer battery life, *and* the ability to dump raw video right into a laptop computer on a desk in the back of a minicam truck, neighborhood mayhem and nighttime crime scene live shots were made for TV. (Over the years, I watched a definite change take place in neighborhood residents. At one time people would enjoy an opportunity to be on television, often jumping up and down behind reporters. But as camera crews became commonplace "in the hood" and were nearly always there because something dreadful had happened, people began to shun being on camera.)

By 2003 or 2004, less than ten years after digital formats were introduced, Internet technology began sweeping into newsrooms. With the popularity of Facebook, Twitter, and other social media newcomers came a revolution in broadcast techniques. Newspapers like the *New York Times, Washington Post, Wall Street Journal,* and the *Chicago Tribune* began expanding their digital operations. This meant that the consumer was able to view or read content right from a computer and do so for free.

But nothing is really free except a mother's love. Newspapers began losing readers, and subscriptions plummeted. Editors and newspapers began looking for ways to expand their Internet operations, hoping to offset the revenue loss by slowly including ads on the web pages and even placing ads on the sacrosanct front page of the newspaper. Television stations also began placing emphasis on web coverage, adding a newly formed position of "electronic journalist" to the staff. Marisa Rodriguez, one of WGN's web producers, says television stations soon learned the importance of having a web presence:

> Twitter, Facebook, all of that is so important nowadays. I mean that's how, sometimes, we find out about stories. Your Twitter [alerts]—you see something trending—you say, "What is this?" And what you [decide is] maybe we should post this on our site. This is trending right now—this is big. So, we put it up there, and we'll tweak our link up with the same story and you should see the numbers. . . . [They] just shoot up with that story.[22]

But while the digital paradigm was still trying to gain a foothold on viewers and readers, the meteoric growth of so-called smartphones began to alter the way news organizations approached getting their product to the public.

Now, the paradigm has shifted again. During the May 20, 2012, NATO summit in Chicago, television stations were able to broadcast live from the demonstration. Using a Dejero box (see chapter seven), reporters and camera crews, marching alongside protestors, were able to send a signal via cell phone or over the Internet directly to the servers in their respective stations and could then broadcast to the public live, unedited reports that brought the event directly into the homes of viewers—raw and sometimes profane. Ten years ago, CNN needed ten suitcases and three people to go live from anywhere. Now, with one cell phone–type Dejero box, a single cameraperson could report live from any spot on the globe as long as there was a cell signal.

In recent years, another innovation has come to the aid of TV newspeople working in remote areas: satellite phones. Although limited in quality, this approach uses satellite audio channels to send highly compressed video signals back to the newsroom.

So during this last one hundred years, the paradigm for disseminating news, information, and entertainment has shifted several times from film to videotape, roughly forty years from 1940 to 1980; from videotape to digital, in the twenty years between 1980 and 2000; and finally from digital to Internet, over the past ten years. And now stations can broadcast via Dejero-type devices that are the current standard for rapid distribution of information.

Today, the ability to transmit live video has shifted again with apps like Periscope or Facebook. Now, anyone with a smartphone can go live, turning his or her own phone into a local TV studio—broadcasting live over the Internet to anyone anywhere in the world.

With Periscope all you need to do is give your topic a title because the app is already connected to all of your contacts. Additionally anyone else who accesses the app can tune in to your broadcast if the person clicks on your title. This allows the public to view your live broadcast.

These progressive paradigm shifts mean that people now have near-instantaneous access to information . . . compared to those from past generations, who had to wait, in some cases, days to learn about an event. So does this rapid, lightning-fast process of flooding us with data and material mean that storytelling is any better? Regrettably, in the vast majority of cases, I think not. As these major shake-ups redefine how news is disseminated, television stations keep chasing the next "shiny" thing on the market—the hottest gadget that's in vogue this month. But the fallacy in quickly jumping from paradigm to paradigm is that these fresh, experimental ways of broadcasting news rarely have an opportunity to develop into sturdy, dependable processes before we are on to the next "new" thing.

Changing technology is wonderful. But when the subsequent method is unreliable, because it was rushed into service, we become dissatisfied with it and seek a better way of doing what was working before. This means that quality control never has an opportunity to be built into the new process. But along the way, in some instances, a new paradigm does manage to stick. The current generation is embracing social media and joining friends by the billions.

Welcome to the blurb generation where people tweet their thoughts in 140 characters or less. The pendulum of communication is swinging away from long-form writing, as the current generation grows more accustomed to the fleeting, choppy thoughts of Facebook, Twitter, Snapchat, and Instagram. In traditional news formats, attempts are made to present both sides equally. According to Marisa Rodriguez,

> I've seen us work it this way: if we do not have a comment from some person, we will say so-and-so chose not to comment at this time, just to make sure. [W]e've had to do that a lot because . . . there are stories that need to be put out there but we do not have both sides. So, what to do, not report it? I think this is the fair way—you call the people, they don't want to comment, and you let people [the audience] know that the person wouldn't comment.[23]

Enthusiasts of mobile devices—cell phones, iPads, and the like—have begun to communicate on a global level, flashing text messages and photos around the planet as easily as your grandmother spoke to her neighbor over the backyard fence. These devices can already receive one language and translate it into another in a split second. So now, billions of people are the readers—the audience—the targets of data and information for good reasons . . . as well as evil intentions.

But once the pendulum of communication reaches the apex it will begin to swing back in the other direction. It always does. At some point our unquenchable thirst for seeking to communicate faster and to more people—with bites, blurbs, and phrases—will fizzle out.

Equilibrium is always the force that keeps humankind from going over the proverbial edge. But until news reporting settles down and producers and assignment editors try to responsibly cover a balanced mixture of stories, some victims will continue to be overlooked because there are more glamorous or prominent subjects to cover.

There may never be a complete return to the classic forms of storytelling. But I doubt that the love of such will ever die. Og, the caveman, probably knew that a well-crafted story is like nothing else. It is able to fill the spirit with exciting and compelling thoughts and images that can last a lifetime.

Today, instead of speaking in a cave, atop a broken stalagmite stump—where Og's voice used to echo off a wall—speakers, now, can tell stories that are heard and seen around the globe in the blink of an eye.

But that paradigm, too, is about to change as quickly as you can turn this page.

Chapter Four

SURVEY—DECIDING WHICH MURDER STORIES TO COVER

T his is the part where you get to put yourself in the shoes of the newsroom gatekeepers. No answers are right or wrong. Those who've read this book have told me that it was fascinating to be able to act and make the same decisions that a real newsroom executive would make. Some of these scenarios are tougher to decide than others; some are pretty simple to resolve. You also may realize something about yourself that you never had admitted before—discovering that you consider some people to be more important than others.

To supplement and substantiate some of the thesis points made in this book, and to learn more about how murder stories are covered in Chicago, I composed and sent out a thirty-three-question survey to assignment editors and show producers at Chicago television stations (they were assured that their identities and television stations would be completely anonymous). This group was selected because their responses would, in all likelihood, reflect the sentiments of editors and producers in other markets across the country.

The rationale for choosing this demographic: Chicago is the third-largest television market in the country.[1] Chicago is a city with a high murder rate (Chicago in 2012 was called the "Murder Capital" of the US). Because of the frequency of murders, editors and producers are proficient in quickly deciding how to cover violent crimes in general and murders in particular. As a major market, Chicago offers journalists all the latest electronic tools necessary for maximizing coverage of murders. Journalists in major markets tend to be more seasoned, as opposed to much smaller markets where journalists are often inexperienced and are right out of school.

Assisting me in this effort were three students in a master's degree program at Loyola University in Chicago. Linlin Wu, Ta Ong, and Andrew Beck were all statistics majors studying in the graduate school. The students were in a course teaching them how to consult as statisticians. As a part of their semester project, they were assigned to work with me to examine the questionnaire I devised and make sure there were as few biases as possible. They also counseled me on the structure of the questions and the forms of questions to be used to extract the most objective conclusions.

All the television stations in Chicago were invited to participate. Only two stations actively engaged their editors and producers to take part, producing forty-one respondents.

This survey was based on an earlier study that I undertook when writing my dissertation.

PILOT STUDY

In June 1995, in preparation for my dissertation, I began a pilot study that was conducted at WGN-TV, using questionnaires. The aim of the study was to gather specific information from the pilot study population, information that dealt with news events to examine any preconceived notions of a prejudicial nature. In this instance the population was newsroom decision makers who determine which stories are covered.[2]

On any given day in newsrooms in Chicago, key personnel make decisions, during breaking stories, on how various murder victims will be "treated" or given priority in subsequent newscasts. Assignment editors and producers are usually the gatekeepers who filter information and make decisions on the content of each newscast. At some point, either in a meeting or an impromptu conference, a decision is made to give a murder story a certain priority. That level of importance may be from presenting the story at the top of the show, along with "sidebar" associated stories, to placing the story after the second or third commercial break or even omitting it altogether.

These decisions are made, in most cases, quickly and matter-of-factly, as though there were unwritten rules that have established a protocol for making the murder of one person more important than that of another. (Likewise, the public seems to acquiesce to these unwritten conventions and seemingly understands why the particular determination was made.)

In presenting television news each day, journalists apply a variety of schemes for selecting from a pool of news stories they have gathered. Of particular interest, to this study, is the importance given to the victims of some murders while other murder victims receive little attention or go unreported altogether.

Studies of news reports have found that news selection involves more than an evaluation of stories according to their news merits. Some researchers have pointed out the role of ideology in decision making. Others have focused on the role of the news organization—its demands, limitations, and resource availabilities—in shaping what is aired. In addition, several studies have found that television news decision making is a group process instead of one made by individuals.

In the case of murder victims, the story usually comes to the attention of the assignment editor as a breaking story. This happens in a number of ways: from a phone tip, over the "wire" from other news sources, from the police radio scanner, or in another competitor's newscast. (When this happens, everybody scrambles to try and play catch-up.)

· If the station that breaks the murder is playing the story as the lead story, then chances are the other stations will do the same. But if a station has exclusive knowledge of a murder, then the status of the story will be automatically elevated because it is thought that sole "ownership" of a story is good for ratings—if the story is exclusive to that particular station and not seen on others. (There is no evidence proving this to be true. Furthermore, viewers usually watch only one station at a time, and if they are watching a newscast on station "A" they don't know what they are missing on station "B.")

Generally, all television stations learn of a murder or murders at about the same time. And, for the most part, all stations seem to give the story the same kind or level of treatment. This accounts for the phenomenon of the same story appearing at the beginning or top of the show on all stations in the same city.

This means that personnel at several television stations are, somehow, using the same "yardstick" for deciding that the murders of some individuals are more important or newsworthy than the murders of others.

In Chicago, between four hundred and a thousand murders are committed each year.[3] Yet television stations on average report no more than two hundred of these crimes. This means that a much greater percentage of murders go unreported than are reported. What happens to make the unreported murders less newsworthy?

Examples of these decisions are commonplace:

- If a prominent doctor or lawyer or teacher is found murdered, he or she will get top-story billing.
- But the murder of a homeless person or ex-convict or illegal alien may not get any news attention.
- A white female, shot to death in an upscale suburb or in a popular location, will be the top story and receive heavy media coverage.

- But a white female shot to death in public housing may go unnoticed.
- A black teenage street gang member killed in a drive-by shooting on the West Side of Chicago will probably not get covered.
- But a black teenage student shot to death on the way to school will surely make the news.
- A woman enters a school in the North Shore (an area where many prominent Chicago suburbs are found) and shoots a student to death. Before the day is over the whole country will know what has happened.
- But when a man, a week later, enters a school on the South Side (in a poor neighborhood) and shoots three people, it will be a big story for only a few days.

In each case a human being was murdered, a senseless loss of life. Yet news organizations routinely apply a sense of urgency to the murders of some people while little or no importance is given to the murders of others.

A clear example of this conscientious effort to highlight some particular murders is the case of O. J. Simpson. This flamboyant, sensational, and melodramatic story saturated the airwaves when it occurred. And now, more than twenty-three years later, it still commands a prime spot in newscasts. The O. J. saga met all the important foci of interest that set a story on the course toward becoming a high-profile case: race, celebrity, wealth, sex, violence, drama, and suspense.

These decisions to "play up" one story and downplay another are consciously made by the gatekeepers (assignment editors and producers) who are motivated by a give-the-viewers-what-they-want mentality. And in most cases they are right. The public does seem to find what it is presented with to be interesting (ratings show this to be true). At least in part, journalists' news selection seems to be the result of schemes for deciding what news is and isn't. And the story will be news for a week.

On the introductory page of my survey, the following instructions were provided for journalists:

This analysis (Pilot Study) will examine some of the variables that exist among assignment editors and producers. The intent is to understand some of these factors and attempt to pinpoint why the murders of some individuals are deemed more important or more interesting than the murders of others.

QUESTIONNAIRE

Murder Stories: How journalists decide which stories to cover.

Purpose of Questionnaire: To examine and understand the process for deciding which murder stories to cover when news breaks.

Given the finite number of crews, on any given weekday, there are always more news stories to cover, in a city like Chicago, than available camera crews and reporters. Assignment editors and producers are the information gatekeepers and decision makers. They filter and decide which murder stories will be covered. Additionally, the analysis will examine the degree to which producers assess each story and decide how it is to be "stacked" in the show. Producers then decide how each story is to be weighted—very important, moderately important, important, not so important, or not worthy of coverage. The survey will be the basis of a chapter in postgraduate study on how journalists in Chicago make decisions when deciding news coverage of murder stories. The subjects of the questionnaire are assignment editors and producers at all Chicago television stations. There are no "correct" or "incorrect" answers. But all answers are important. Once compiled, the data will be analyzed and distributed to the television stations for your use. We urge you to complete the survey and return it. The closer we are to 100 percent of producers and assignment editors in Chicago will add to the accuracy of the study. The survey is completely anonymous. There is no way for researchers to know your identity or the station where you are employed. The survey should take less than ten minutes to complete.

Of the forty-one respondents who completed the questionnaire, there were almost equal demographic representations among assignment editors and producers. Among assignment editors, 50 percent were male, and 50 percent were female. Of the producers, there were slightly more females than males—54 percent female to 46 percent male. There were also twice as many producers as assignment editors—twenty-eight producers and fourteen editors. (Apparently one person checked both categories, causing the total to equal forty-two.)

The respondents represented a highly educated profile: 95 percent completed college, 4 percent did some graduate work, and 23 percent completed graduate school. The majority of the journalists (71 percent) were white; 17 percent were African American, and 9 percent were listed as other. Almost 3 percent checked "Native Hawaiian or Other Pacific Islander."

The ages of the journalists fell mostly toward being young adult to middle age: 17.5 percent in the 25–34 age group, 35 percent in the 35–44 age group, 19 percent who were 45–54, and 10 percent who were 55–64. Only one person fell in the 65–74 age group. One person was over 75, and one person was under 24.

Finally, on the question of politics, there was a rather broad spectrum of ideology. The choices ranged from extremely liberal to extremely conservative: 9.7 percent listed as extremely liberal; 31.7 percent (the majority) listed as moderately liberal; 17.7 percent listed as slightly liberal; 19.5 percent, the second-largest group, were neither liberal nor conservative; 14.6 percent were slightly conservative; and, finally, 7.3 percent were moderately conservative.

The first part of the survey consisted of scenarios that were designed to be difficult to answer. That is because the editors and producers must decide which scenario is the more important of the two. It would force them to decide which person or location or neighborhood (black or white, inner city or suburban) was more significant. In this first set of scenarios, the assignment editors had to decide between a black inner-city neighborhood and a predominately white suburban area. Since the editors are very familiar with all parts of the city and suburbs, there was no need to reference race in the scenarios—it was implied by the locations.

In this section, through the use of scenarios—describing situations surrounding different murders—respondents will be asked to decide on each potential story and judge the merits of each: which one should be covered and to what extent?

SCENARIO #1: Tuesday afternoon, when there is a full complement of staff at work: most are out in the street covering news, but one reporter and camera crew are still in the newsroom waiting for an assignment. There are two simultaneous phone calls to the assignment desk.

Caller: A teenaged gangbanger just ran into the park and shot another gang member—I know he is dead. They have been shooting over here on the West Side all week—I don't know when it's going to stop. It's just crazy!

At the same time, there is another call to the desk.

Caller: A man just walked into an apartment house here in Hinsdale and shot a woman—I'm sure she's dead. He then walked out the door and drove away. We seldom get any crime in this neighborhood. This is just crazy.

The assignment editor confers with the EP (executive producer)

of the next show. You have to get the crew out the door as quickly as possible. Editor and producer talk and make a decision. Where do you send the reporter and crew?

In talking with assignment editors and producers who had hesitated to complete the survey, some felt that having to make a decision was unfair. Because in the *real* world, they said they would have, somehow, covered both stories. A respondent comment:

> While I answered your questions, there is no REAL way to choose between some of these scenarios. We would have to cover BOTH equally. There should have been an option for BOTH, not just either/or. There are many factors that go into deciding what story to cover and how to cover it.

But I related to them (in terms of this survey) that one situation would have to be selected *first* if there was only one reporter and cameraperson in the newsroom at the time. And that would, to some extent, determine their leanings toward feeling that one victim was more important than another.

And in support of the editors who complained about having to make a selection: it is true that in a real-life situation, when two major stories broke out simultaneously, editors and producers would find a way to get both stories covered and not ignore one because of another. So the criticism from the editors and producers is legitimate. One respondent left these remarks in the comment section:

> In news it's never a matter of one murder or another. You can cover both; however, one may be without a reporter. Logistics play a key role. Can a reporter get to the murder site in time for a live shot? That figures into the equation as well.

But I wanted to use the scenarios as a means of determining if there would be a tendency to think of one area as being more important than another. And the numbers do show a very strong bias: in the first scenario, 95 percent listed the suburban apartment house and 5 percent said the (African American) West Side park. Another respondent felt the survey forced answers that were unrealistic:

> As an assignment editor, many of these questions were difficult to answer because the scenarios presented are not usually that clear cut. There are gray areas that influence what gets covered, etc. In addition there are other resources that influence what gets covered—i.e., stringers, LNS [local news service]. So sometimes when there is just one crew, that doesn't necessarily mean we will ignore another important story. We just might have to use different resources to get something covered.

Scenario #2 produced some possibly interesting results. The scenario presented the editors and producers with two important elements—race of subjects and locations of crimes. The choice was between a prominent, world-class shopping district versus a park where mostly African Americans congregate.

SCENARIO #2: Tuesday afternoon, when there is a full complement of staff at work: most are out in the street covering news, but one reporter and camera crew are still in the newsroom waiting for an assignment. There are two simultaneous phone calls to the assignment desk.

Caller: Someone just walked into the Suave Bar and Grill on Michigan Avenue and hacked up several people with a machete. The owner told me one woman was killed and six others were injured— one man lost a hand. There is blood all over the place. People ran out into the street screaming in a panic. It was horrible. I've never seen so much carnage. Michigan Avenue has been shut down, and there are cops everywhere.

At the same time there is another call to the desk.

Caller: There is a gang war going on over here in Jackson Park.

Somebody just rolled by in a van, opened the door, and shot into a crowd of people. He was using a semiautomatic weapon. The policeman told me two people are dead and several others have been injured. There is blood all over the place. People were running and screaming in panic. It was horrible. I've never seen so much carnage. King Drive has been shut down, and there are cops everywhere.

Where do you send the reporter and crew?

In this instance, the differences of opinion reflected almost exactly along the lines of the number of respondents listed as white and black. Twenty-nine of the respondents listed themselves as white, and seven listed themselves as African American. Thirty-three thought Michigan Avenue was the more important story; eight saw Jackson Park (the black park) as more important.

Does this mean that individuals in different ethnic groups think stories that more closely pertain to them and their everyday lives are more important? A look at the variable of race should be examined.

Another scenario was even tougher to decide. It examined who among two groups of bad guys produced a better or more important story.

SCENARIO #3: Producers and assignment editors who come to work on a Monday morning are handed two newspapers as sources of good stories to cover and do in-depth reporting, seeking answers. A community newspaper in the NW suburbs runs a front-page story about a huge problem that has caught the attention of the governor. A motorcycle gang has been at war with a rival motorcycle gang over the distribution of methamphetamine and heroin in the NW suburban area. High school kids are dropping like flies—six high school students have died, and several others are in the hospital from a "bad" or deadly batch of meth. Four gang members—two from each gang—have also been murdered in the war.

Local residents are frantic, not knowing what to do and fearing that their kids are in danger. Police say they are working on leads but don't have much else to go on and can't stop this growing problem.

The second newspaper (on the West Side) has this story that has caught the attention of the governor: A street gang has been at war with a rival neighborhood gang over the distribution of methamphetamine and heroin on the Humboldt Park area in the West Side. High school kids are dropping like flies—six high school students have died, and several others are in the hospital from a bad batch of heroin. Four gang members—two from each gang—have also been murdered in the war. Local residents are frantic, not knowing what to do and fearing that their kids are in danger. Police say they are working on leads but don't have much to go on and can't stop this growing problem. Where do you send the reporter and crew?

The West Side street gang gained slightly more importance, 53 percent to the suburban motorcycle gang, 47 percent. Clearly journalists were almost evenly divided as to which group would be the better story—although there were five respondents who skipped this question and the rest of the other scenarios. This probably skewed the results just a bit.

Scenario #4 was developed to examine the rationale for choosing one location over another. In the two incidents, editors and producers were asked to choose which murder story would have the greater impact when both were equally violent, yet one involved middle-class immigrants in a neighborhood setting while the other involved wealthy immigrants in a popular upscale restaurant.

SCENARIO #4: Police send out two alerts. Two longtime buddies immigrated to the US from Juarez, Mexico. After twenty years of struggling and building their business, they became successful and built a multimillion-dollar chain of seventeen auto repair shops located in poor neighborhoods throughout the city. When one partner wanted to buy out the other partner, a heated exchange developed over dinner one night in an upscale Mexican restaurant, resulting in a violent confrontation. One man pulled a gun and began shooting. His partner was killed, and three innocent patrons were

wounded in the gunfire. In the second alert, two longtime buddies immigrated to the US from Toronto, Canada. After twenty years of struggling and building their business, they became successful and built a multimillion-dollar chain of tax consultant offices located in the Gold Coast (upscale Chicago neighborhood) and the Chicago Board of Trade. When one partner wanted to buy out the other partner, a heated exchange developed over dinner one night in an upscale high-rise restaurant, resulting in a violent confrontation. One man pulled a gun and began shooting. His partner was killed, and three innocent patrons were wounded in the gunfire. Where do you send the reporter and crew?

The vast majority of respondents, 80 percent, felt the upscale restaurant made for a more important story, while 20 percent felt the incident in the neighborhood eatery was more important. Clearly, location where a murder occurs is a prime factor in deciding how to cover murder victims.

Scenario #5 examined how editors and producers would feel when having to decide which murder to cover if the victims were elderly women or toddlers. By an overwhelming margin of 92 percent to 8 percent, respondents chose toddlers as being the more important murder stories.

SCENARIO #5: Assignment editors monitoring scanners hear two reports of shootings, both with confirmed fatalities.

Call #1: Cop: Shots fired in a store for young mothers on Touhy in Niles—two four-year-old children confirmed dead on scene. Suspect—white, male, dressed in black body armor from head to foot. Suspect fled on red motorbike.

Call #2: Cop: Shots fired in a senior retirement apartment building on W. Peterson and Ridge—two eighty-year-old women confirmed dead on scene. Suspect—white, male, dressed in black body armor from head to foot. Suspect fled on red motorbike.

Where do you send the reporter and crew?

In this scenario, even with five respondents choosing not to answer, it is quite apparent that the sentiment toward the importance of small children as murder victims is, without a doubt, almost always going to be chosen as the more important story. Throughout the questionnaire there is a very strong feeling in favor of the importance of small children over other victims.

And while elderly murder victims do sometimes rank higher than younger adults, other factors often come into play such as the following: Was the older person helpless, or taken advantage of? Was the elderly person homeless? Had he or she been ill for an extended period of time? These seem to be mitigating factors that can move the older murder victim either up or down the ladder of importance. But small children, because of their innocence and vulnerability, almost always rank very high on the scale of importance.

Scenario #7 again points out that *location* is deemed to be an important determinant when selecting which murder stories to cover. In this case, both victims were immigrant women, killed by a family member. The only differentiating element was location: one was killed in an ethnic neighborhood while the other was killed in a busy downtown business district. By a two-to-one margin, the downtown location was selected as being the most important story—66.5 percent to 33.5 percent.

There was a near-unanimous selection in scenario #8. Respondents were asked to examine two sets of African American teens—both groups were innocent victims—with the goal to learn more about the perception that some victims are more important than others. I think this might be the most significant finding in the study.

SCENARIO #8: Five black teens are standing on a street corner at Pulaski and Twenty-Second Street. They are shooting dice when someone from a passing van shoots and kills two of the teens. Police say the boys are connected to a gang. . . . Five black teens are walking to school at Pulaski and Twenty-First Street. They are laughing and

discussing basketball when someone from a passing van shoots and kills two of the teens. Police say the boys are not connected to a gang. Where do you send the reporter and crew?

By a landslide margin of 94 percent to 6 percent, respondents felt the black kids walking to school would make the more important story. Both groups were innocent victims and hadn't committed a crime, but because one group was referred to by police as being in a gang and the other group was not, the boys walking to school were deemed by a large majority to be the more important story. The other boys were "throwaway" kids, not felt to be significant enough to be given news coverage because of the stereotypical negative connotation of being in a gang.

But why was there such a strong sentiment toward the kids walking to school over the kids shooting dice? And even though the answers reflect a strong bias toward one group over another, one respondent was unapologetically critical that such distinctions should even be examined in the first place:

> I find the first set of either/or questions to be extremely problematic. In each case, we would bust an already assigned reporter to cover the so-called "b" story in addition to the "a" story. In other words, there is no either/or in those questions. I've covered news for fifteen years, and I can't recall a day where I've had to choose either/or in such extreme scenarios. In those cases, you find a way to cover both. In each instance, it was an effort to push a user towards a story that has more unique circumstances (read: more affluent) versus a story of the same merit that happens much more often. If the goal is to prove that newspeople cover violent crime in affluent areas more aggressively, point proven; but it's an act of small-minded academic masturbation. You don't need a study to realize that—and the conclusions are obvious. I can't imagine those questions standing up to any level of serious academic scrutiny. They're so basic and biased that I was almost embarrassed

answering them. The ranking questions were more interesting, as they acknowledge that news operates in different shades of gray. Perhaps I'm trying to think beyond the survey, but I wonder what new ground is going to be broken by any of this.

While comments like this one are welcomed, it does seem that questions aimed at uncovering personal preconceptions about race and socioeconomic standing touch sensitive nerves. On the other hand, the act of trying to uncover private biases is apt to force editors and producers to admit that their long-established "unwritten" gut feelings about which news stories get covered, automatically, and which ones sometimes fall by the wayside, need to be reexamined.

Question 18: When covering murder stories, who do you think the audience (viewers) is most interested in learning about: the victim or the suspect?

There was a wide margin of sentiment among the respondents: 80 percent thought the victim was more important, and 20 percent felt the suspect was a more interesting element in a story. And by that same margin, on the next question, editors and producers felt that the race of the victim was *not* a deciding factor in choosing which story to cover—80 percent said no, while 20 percent felt race was a factor when making a choice in which story to cover. (The race of respondents might reveal interesting results if that data is correlated, looking at this question.)

Question 19: Does the race of the victim ever affect your decisions in giving priority to one story over another?

The answers covered a wide range: 80 percent said no, while 20 percent said yes. Again, since the percentages reflect the same ratio as the numbers of white to black respondents, it might be enlightening to cross-check the replies against the races of the respondents.

Question 20: Please indicate your thoughts and feelings about the variables below and how important each is to the selection of

murder stories that are covered: gender, age, race (of victim), location, prominence, race (of suspect).

Editors and producers leaned toward (in order) prominence, location, and age as the leading elements in determining the importance of a murder story. The race of the victim and suspect were about even and least important among all the factors.

Question 23 looked at the ranking of importance among Hispanic male murder victims. A gang member ranked the lowest while a Hispanic police officer ranked the highest. A Hispanic lawn-care worker ranked third while a CTA bus driver came in last. The answers from the respondents show a consistently negative perception toward gang members and a positive feeling toward police officers or authority figures.

Question 25 looked at *location* from a mostly social-economic standpoint, comparing the importance of communities if a murder were to occur there.

Question 25: If you have to make a choice among five locations, please rank the following "story elements" (dealing with murder location). Rank in order of influence or importance (1 being most important, 5 being the least).

The high-crime African American neighborhood of Englewood was thought to be the least important while the affluent, upscale Lincoln Park neighborhood ranked the highest.

Question 29 inquired about the feelings of respondents toward the importance of socioeconomic status of the victim:

Does the socioeconomic level of the victim affect your decisions in giving priority to one story over another?

Both groups were almost even: 51 percent said no, while 49 percent replied yes. But these figures conflict with earlier responses where more affluent neighborhoods were often chosen over ghetto or inner-city areas populated by poor minorities.

Questions 32 and 33 examined the differences in importance between the race of the victim and the race of the suspect.

Question 32: Does the race of the victim strongly influence your decision on covering a murder?

Question 33: Does the race of the suspect strongly influence your decision on covering a murder?

Data from both questions were almost identical: 85 percent said no, while 15 percent said yes.

CONCLUSION

At the outset it should be noted that very little new ground was uncovered. But several theoretical suspicions were confirmed—at least among these respondents.

I believe journalists responded to the survey in an honest and forthright effort to answer the questions as truthfully as the structure of the survey permitted them to be. They were, as many complained, restricted from deciding how to creatively cover many scenarios, as they might have if simultaneous murder situations had developed. But, in the name of scientific study, the questionnaire as constructed was designed to extract immediate and impulsive reactions to contrasting situations, which might lead to some observable trends in the conclusions they (the journalists) drew.

Among this group of respondents, it is clear that some of the elements produce nearly unanimous feelings that go into deciding which murders to cover: the murder of an infant or a toddler will almost always be covered as a top priority; *location* of any murder is deemed as an important determinant in deciding which murder to cover; a murder in an upscale location frequented by individuals from an upper socioeconomic bracket will usually trump a murder scene in a poor or ethnic area. When a murder occurs, editors and producers are more interested in the victim than the perpetrator (unless there are outstanding factors concerning the suspect, i.e., age, extreme political views, unusual motivations, etc.). The vast majority of editors and producers do not consider race when deciding the importance of contrasting murder stories.

The data gathered from this study can be useful to help prevent assignment editors and producers from approaching news in a cookie-cutter fashion. Too often snap decisions are made in an effort to rapidly disseminate news to viewers, when just a moment more of inquiry might uncover a much better story that would have ordinarily been overlooked. But it will become increasingly difficult for assignment editors to resist the immense pressure to quickly shoot crews out the door instead of pausing a few moments to look for a deeper or more compelling hook on which to hang the story.

Most assignment editors are not daring or seasoned enough to withstand the pressure from certain show producers, whose most overriding motivation is to fill his or her show with content and not be concerned with the quality or worth of the story, or both. (Show producers are, in fact, very interested in the content of the stories, but their need to fill a time period with stories is an overriding consideration. You can bet they are not going to elect to fill a show with color bars because they refused to put on inferior content.)

Additionally, editors and producers must hesitate to allow coverage of news to be routine. News is, itself, chaotic and unpredictable. A murder story is mitigated by so many circumstances that no two murders are the same. So murder stories and their coverage should not be looked upon as identical—instances of crime never are. But since news routines can become habitual, editors and producers must struggle against the tendency to view murder coverage as customary or typical.

Chapter Five

GOOD GUYS VS. BAD GUYS

A boxing match is like a cowboy movie. There's got to be good guys and there's got to be bad guys. And that's what people pay for—to see the bad guys get beat.

—Sonny Liston,
former heavyweight boxing champion

Amid the "calls to action" to stop the shootings and murders in Chicago is the realization that no one has so far come up with a workable solution—and that is horrifying. The block-by-block street gangs are caught up in retaliations and vendettas that loop back and forth like a self-proliferating feud that will only end when all the members have run out of bullets or have wiped each other out.

Seasoned news gatekeepers know each day that sometime before their shift ends, police radios will crackle with the always-chilling pronouncement, "Shots fired, shots fired! Multiple victims at the scene." I have no doubt that gatekeepers cringe knowing that something awful had just happened—perhaps a loss of lives. Yet I would guess that many assignment editors and producers have become jaded, world weary, and worn out. Even though they love their work, no one likes to constantly observe the unceasing drumbeat of senseless murders.

Humans—even, and perhaps especially, gang members—are social creatures. From the moment we are born we must have someone else's help or we would perish. Unlike some animals that hatch from eggs and are entirely independent once they free themselves from the shell, we are completely helpless from the first breath—and even that sometimes only happens because of the aid of another human being. We thrive on being a part of the group.

When our ancestors—the earliest mammals—appeared on the scene some two hundred million years ago, the evolution of the species reorganized the ties that families have. Babies came into the world as limp, helpless creatures unable to lift their own heads. In order to survive, they needed warmth, nourishment, and protection, given to them by their parents. That reliance is as necessary today as it was millions of years ago. For a mammalian infant, the largest threat or danger did not come from an attacker or predator, but it came from being left alone—unattended to die in the wild. Although some higher species are loners, the majority live in bands, packs, pods, troops, or prides. They rely on one another for protection, grooming, food, and all the necessities of life. These are the same social requirements that bind gang members together.

And this is the tricky part: in order to live in a singular group, social animals need a way to smooth over the endless array of potential conflicts and compromises that can arise when multiple individuals have to share the same space and resources; there are real benefits and drawbacks. But gang members who are never taught how to tiptoe around the dangers of disagreements use handguns rather than compromise when conflict arises.

Arthur Schopenhauer, the German philosopher, came up with the "hedgehog's dilemma" (or sometimes the porcupine's dilemma), which is a parable about the challenges of human intimacy:

> A number of porcupines huddled together for warmth on a cold day in winter; but, as they began to prick one another with their quills, they were obliged to disperse. However the cold drove them together again, when just the same thing happened. At last, after many turns of huddling and dispersing, they discovered that

they would be best off by remaining at a little distance from one another. In the same way the need of society drives the human porcupines together, only to be mutually repelled by the many prickly and disagreeable qualities of their nature. The moderate distance which they at last discover to be the only tolerable condition of intercourse, is the code *of politeness and fine manners*, and those who transgress it are roughly told—in the English phrase—to keep their distance. By this arrangement the mutual need of warmth is only very moderately satisfied; but then, people do not get pricked. A man who has some heat in himself prefers to remain outside, where he will neither prick other people nor get pricked himself.[1]

If you don't think this is true, try walking up to someone you know and walk very close, almost nose to nose. That person will step back and look at you in amazement because you would have crossed an unspoken barrier and moved into what we consider "personal space." Subconsciously—and consciously in the case of strangers—that person would exhibit signs of fear, wondering why you were so dangerously near. Our ancient ancestors learned that very close proximity for anyone was a perilous practice to allow.[2] With a friend or foe less than an arm's length from us, our defenses would be compromised; we couldn't flee or fight very well. So over the millennia we have adopted the habits of not allowing our personal space to be violated.

In his book *Extreme Fear: The Science of Your Mind in Danger*, Jeff Wise discusses how great apes, including human beings, have a much more complicated social network, one that includes things like kinship bonds and shifting alliances. But the principle is the same: anytime new individuals come into the group, they have to find their place within it, a procedure that involves challenging others and either submitting to them or dominating them. Wise says this process is so deeply ingrained that it goes on subconsciously, through gesture and posture and tone of voice. Rituals like saying hello, shaking hands, asking "How are you?" and hugging good-bye are all actions that, though we carry them out automatically, are reflections of an ancient subconscious system for maintaining our social position.[3]

Street gang members have developed a complex system of hand signs and symbols, colors and slogans, to distinguish themselves from their enemies. Members flash finger signs to both warn their rivals and welcome their friends. Find yourself unable to answer correctly with a counter hand sign and you will bear the wrath of an angry foe.

This need to congregate in groups of like-minded individuals and people who look alike, who are from the same ethnic group or religious sect, or who speak the same language is a common, everyday occurrence that happens from a need for security and a need for convenience. The first question immigrants have when they land in a new country is "Where are the rest of us?" They know once they find the "neighborhood," life for them will improve. They will be able to verbally express themselves to others who will understand what they are saying. They will find specific types of foods that they used to eat back home. Their religious needs can also be met as, chances are, a gathering place for services will be nearby. But there are also complexities of survival that are a microcosm of the larger society.

In a classic scene from the 1974 movie *The Godfather: Part II*, a young Vito Corleone (during a flashback to his youth) is asked by a friend of his wife's to please come to her aid. The old woman is being threatened with eviction by a reprehensible character named Signor Roberto. The old lady has a dog, and the landlord uses the animal as an excuse to evict her because he can get more money from the next tenants.[4]

Vito asks Signor Roberto to please permit the old lady to remain in the apartment as a favor to him . . . telling Roberto to ask around the neighborhood about Vito to learn that Vito was a person to be trusted. Signor Roberto all but spits in Vito's face, but after learning about Vito killing a despicable freelance "black hand" extortionist, the landlord returns to Vito's office and offers to let the old lady remain in the apartment at reduced rents.

While this is a fictionalized account of events that took place at the turn of the century, it nonetheless shows how life for new immigrants in America was a complicated, tough time during which these poor, mostly uneducated émigrés barely eked out an existence. Yet, they remained in their ghettos and raised generations in neighborhoods that were Italian or Irish or Greek or Jewish or black.

Unemployment was high, gangs ruled the neighborhoods, and crime—mostly perpetrated by people living in the area on people living there—was rampant. Outsiders rarely ventured into the neighborhood. It sounds exactly like many urban areas in big cities today.

Inner-city neighborhoods of today have become so oppressive and so dangerous that children seldom venture outside their own yards to play. I remember, years ago, driving through West Side neighborhoods and seeing kids riding bikes, skating, boys running around the block, and one of the joys of summer—girls jumping rope. We used to stop our crew car to watch girls jump double Dutch.[5] Today on a bright, sunny day, you can drive for blocks and never see a single group of girls jumping rope. The children are inside. The question is, have they stopped going outside because they are at home watching television, playing video games, and on computers, or is it because the threat of violent crime is too imminent? Are the children like young porcupines still trying to determine their proper places, searching to find a secure spot inside the house or in the yard?

Historically, if new immigrants were to begin moving out into broader society, they needed to find employment. They took with them an apprehension or fear that caused them to be cautious. Along the way they could run into religious or ethnic prejudice—negative encounters they may have heard of but never seen in person.

The members of the different groups of individuals, who may have been more dominant in the social pecking order, were also sticking close together, relying on their combined strengths to maintain their superiority. This socioeconomic grouping of individuals is different than the ethnic differentiation, but the result is the same: continued control over one group by another group.

This type of grouping is so highly evolved that subgroups or cliques comprise the many factions that make up all major groups. Even cliques have their own mini-clusters—the elites and the seekers, the haves and the have-nots.

Street gangs have also evolved over the years, becoming more militaristic. Older leaders exert an iron fist over younger, more impressionable members. Strict codes for joining involve ritualistic patterns that indoctrinate new recruits into behaving with a zombie-like loyalty that will allow them to be ordered to do anything the leaders command. That misdirected allegiance makes members robotic soldiers who can be told to kill without question, without remorse.

SOCIETIES BUILD BORDERS

Throughout the years, strategies have developed for keeping one group dominant over another. In housing, for instance, one method of keeping certain ethnic groups cordoned off was dubbed "redlining." Redlining was the practice of denying, or charging more for, services such as banking, insurance, access to healthcare, or even supermarkets—or denying jobs to residents, often in racially determined areas. Banks in many major cities like Chicago were cited for this practice in the sixties, seventies, and eighties. The term "redlining" was coined in the late 1960s by John McKnight, a sociologist and community activist.[6] It refers to the practice of marking a red line on a map to delineate the area where banks would not invest; later the term was applied to discrimination against a particular group of people (usually by race or sex), irrespective of geography. During the heyday of redlining, the areas most frequently discriminated against were black inner-city neighborhoods.

Yet, while this book was being written, a Federal Reserve study called "Race, Redlining, and Subprime Loan Pricing," by Andra C. Ghent, Ruben Hernandez-Murillo, and Michael T. Owyang, indicated that a form of redlining was still going on:

> We investigated whether race and ethnicity influenced subprime loan pricing during 2005, the peak of the subprime mortgage expansion. We combined loan-level data on the performance of non-prime securitized mortgages with individual- and neighborhood-level data on racial and ethnic characteristics for metropolitan areas in California and Florida. Using a model of rate determination that accounts for predicted loan performance, we evaluated the presence of disparate impact and disparate treatment discrimination in mortgage rates. We found evidence of redlining and adverse pricing for blacks and Hispanics. The evidence of adverse pricing was strongest for purchase mortgages and mortgages originated by non-depository institutions.[7]

Banks were quick to counter that they had to be selective on where they offered loans, in order to remain in business—that minority neighborhoods were on the decline and to offer loans in those areas would be too risky. But banks owned by minorities, or small banks struggling to gain a foothold in low-income neighborhoods, did continue to offer loans in uncertain areas—heretofore redlined by major banks. And the neighborhood banks remained in business.

Downtown bankers lacked the sensitivity to understand that ethically there was a rationale for providing loans and not letting whole communities deteriorate. This allowed a cancer of decay and neglect to eat away at entire sections of inner cities. Big banks did not perceive these neighborhoods to be economically important.

MURDER IN THE NEWS

Over the decades, some—not all—inner-city neighborhoods became breeding grounds for crime. These troubled areas became worse as remaining businesses closed shop and left. The first to go were banks, then manufacturing plants, followed by grocery stores, pharmacies, dry cleaners, and service stations. In their places remained liquor stores, convenience stores, currency exchanges, and an occasional fast food restaurant. The main industry fueling this unhealthy and substandard economy was and continues to be drugs.

Street gangs are the conduits through which illegal drugs are sold to addicts and recreational users. It's big business, prompting gang leaders to fight without mercy for precious "turf" where business is conducted.

LEARNING TO SPOT THE "OTHERS"

Perception is mostly driven by contrast, and we largely evaluate ourselves and determine our sense of identity by comparing who we are with others. There are two main ways of doing this: making ourselves appear superior or making others appear inferior. Demonizing others uses the latter method. We'll discuss this more in detail in a later chapter.

Another method of separating ourselves from others is to polarize, making both "us" and "them" more extreme. This creates space between us, making us distinctively different. When people are completely different from us, it is easy to objectify them, converting them into "things" that can be treated in inhuman ways.[8]

Stereotypes are tools used to make generalizations about a group of people whereby we attribute a defined set of characteristics to this group; these classifications can be positive or negative. News producers think of "audience" in different ways and load or stack their shows accordingly, knowing that a different demographic is watching at a particular time. When asked about this, WGN-TV assistant news director and former morning show executive producer Sandy Pudar says,

> You know, it really depends on the hour of the show—in the early-morning hours it's a little more Chicago centric. And a little more later in the mornings . . . we'll be a little bit more national than we are in some of the early hours. Maybe you think that you will cover a sensational national case for a missing woman, a little bit more than you would a house fire. So, you do take into consideration what the audience would be at that hour. So, what we call the little stories . . . that kind of develop overnight . . . kind of lose their way in the later hours. . . . [Y]ou don't see as many house fires— it's ridiculous, but someone who's shot might not make it in the eight o'clock hour of the show. Because by that time the audience is changing . . . moms are getting off to school, and they don't want to hear all the bad news that there is out there. So, you're trying to shape your show a little differently.[9]

Clearly thoughts of the audience play a role in how Pudar and her producers stack the news blocks hour after hour. Saying that moms don't want to hear about violence as they get their children off to school is a form of stereotyping or pigeonholing. We do this both as individuals and also as groups. Within a group, this adds social confirmation and power of agreement by others. A common agreement is that street gangs are a menace and the people in these gangs are less than human. We dehumanize the culprits rather than seeking them out to try and gain a better understanding of what motivates them to act. Not only do we think ourselves superior, but others also tell us we are superior. This is a significant benefit of groups and is a key reason why we attach our identities to the identity of the group. Father Michael Pfleger sees this targeted disparity all the time. He wonders why journalists allow themselves to continue perpetrating myths about different groups or races of people:

> [W]e have become a society that determines that some people's lives are more important than other people's lives. And I think how the media has been part of creating that perception . . . and how it's sold in media reports so people don't think whether it's true or not true. So, they [the media] have become coconspirators, in my mind, with this . . . mentality that life is more valuable in different parts of the city, and among different races and classes of people.[10]

But sometimes, people in groups, teams, and organizations may be tempted to leave and join competitors. This is particularly common in businesses where job seekers may get more money, greater status, and better job prospects. Demonizing other groups acts as a dissuasive warning to members of an opposing group, both that the other person's grass is not greener and that if they leave for the competitor they will be personally demonized by their former friends and colleagues.

Groups often frame outsiders in a negative light, seeing them as less intelligent, less able, and even bad or evil in some way. This is typically done when other groups are viewed as being competitors of some kind. The criticism may not just be of other groups. It may also be of the typical person in the other groups and perhaps even of specific key people within their organization.

The trivialization and demonizing of others is often done in a ritualistic way, using the same words and following established and repeated patterns and sequences. In newsrooms, reporters, assignment editors, and producers often refer to certain neighborhood areas—known to be home to specific minorities—with terms that diminish the importance of what has just occurred: "The shooters were gangbangers," "That's a gang block," "That murder was obviously a 'domestic,'" "He is a repeat offender," or "That's a tough neighborhood." This type of "code" is used frequently, and the inference is that the victim, who may fit one of those terms, is not worthy of being covered or is less important. Father Pfleger has fought the importation of guns and drugs, and stores that sell drug paraphernalia, into his parish. Pfleger has gained a national reputation for turning around his South Side community. He says perceptions can become reality:

> And unfortunately the larger masses begin to look at the folks in those areas that they are just violent folks. But, that perception carries all the way down to the people who live in that area. If people tell you, you are a violent community—you're going to continue to play into those violent hands. Just like: if I tell my son you're stupid, you're stupid, you're stupid—he is going to become stupid. People, unfortunately, are influenced by what you tell them. If you keep telling people they are gangbangers, they act like gangbangers. If you keep telling people in certain communities that [they] are a violent community, then violence becomes an acceptable way of life. So, I think, unfortunately, the system—and I think the media has become coconspirators in this—is determining that certain areas are violent, that certain areas are beyond help, that that's the way it is there, and I think you've had people, unconsciously, playing into their hands.[11]

This repeated trivialization of serious events like murders allows newspeople to disregard events in certain areas and not fret over decisions to forget about human dignity of the victims—the framing of others as less than those in one's own group. WGN-TV managing or planning editor Pat Curry admits that he often has to remind himself that shooters are human, too:

> I set up a story in which it turns out the victim of a homicide was a gangbanger. And I talked to the family—and a lot of times I call the families and sometimes they call here—and I remember speaking to the mother, and she said, "You know, my boy was no angel. He was in a gang. But you know what? He was still a human being." And that really touched me, and I sent a reporter out on that, and I looked at that and I said, "You know, they are human beings too."[12]

This use of code is "just below the line" and is close to being disparaging. It enables the gatekeepers to filter out the "others" just because certain areas may be more crime-ridden. It does not mean that the journalists are prejudiced or racist in any way—*the code terms just make it easier to discuss potentially sensitive subjects and rationalize why those victims are being ignored.* Still, that doesn't mean the crime is any less important—if anything, the higher frequency of murders should prompt management to decide to investigate the regularity of the murders instead of ignoring them because they happen so often.

This form of stereotyping of potential news victims can be subconscious, where it subtly biases our decisions and actions, even in people who consciously do not want to be biased. Yet stereotyping often happens in everyone, not so much because of aggressive or unkind thoughts. It is more often a simplification to speed conversation on what is not considered to be an important topic.

Psychiatrist Carl Bell isn't surprised that journalists have a tacit feeling that some murder victims are more important than others:

> Well, there's this feeling that some people are more important than others, and that is complex because this is America. And in America we're supposed to judge people by the content of their character, not the color of their skin. The problem is that we're all human and as human beings we all had survival mechanisms in our brain— fight, flight, or freeze—which is the limbic system of the amygdala. It's still there, always in operation, and what they do is . . . if someone's different, uneducated, different color, different religion, different language, different sexual orientation—anything they are not, or the "other"—they are the alien, near the door, the nasty, they are the reprehensible.[13]

Journalists are trained to look for and be sensitive to the possibility of stereotyping in their own writing. When we speak among our closest friends—people with whom we have no fear of crossing bounds—we often allow, sometimes in jest, thoughts and revelations to creep out that would be thought to be racist or politically incorrect (PIC) by others who don't know us well. A sarcastic or cynical remark (used by journalists in our "backstage" conversations) could have a withering effect on other people if they were to hear how we speak.

I must admit that I, too, am guilty of using caustic speech—when talking with my colleagues—saying things, often in jest, that I would not dare utter in a public setting. Sadly, this behind-the-scenes "group speech" occurs in most organizations that have developed an internal lexicon or nomenclature.

Chapter Six
BAD GUYS VS. BAD GUYS

We are born of risen apes, not fallen angels.
—Robert Ardrey, anthropologist

In every society, some individuals are tempted to cheat and kill and succumb to selfish impulses. We have dubbed them the bad guys. And because of the antisocial actions of these wrongdoers, they are despised and loathed. So for the rest of us to survive in the presence of these lawbreakers and killers, we need to make this bad behavior costly. And we do, by trying to arrest and put them away as quickly as possible.

And while journalists follow and chronicle the processes of convicting some criminals, others never get public scrutiny. Newsroom jargon in morning and afternoon meetings refers to the shooters as "bad guys" or "gangbangers." This indicates that the gatekeepers are already looking at them in a negative fashion.

Veteran journalists know that the criminal justice system makes it difficult for lawmakers to look objectively on some suspects, even though they are supposed to be considered innocent until proven guilty. (The exceptions to this are the many reporters who toil tirelessly in the Innocence Project—working to free men and women, many of whom have been incarcerated for many years for crimes they did not commit.)

The refusal to "snitch" on neighborhood wrongdoers by those who may know what happened hinders police in catching the perpetrators before they can injure more people. Authorities bump into this wall of secrecy all the time. They find it frustrating that this code of silence exists.

And many times police discover that witnesses "go silent" and don't even offer help—including the victims who were, themselves, injured. Retired Chicago police first deputy superintendent Al Wysinger has had some experience with this:

> Unfortunately, with the culture that's going on in society today, if the bad guys shoot a bad guy—you have that mantra where you hear, as police, "we'll handle this ourselves." Like the violence spike we saw in 2012—I mean, we actually had guys that had been shot at . . . and knew who shot them, but would not tell [us] because of the macho—"I'll take care of this myself" [attitude]. There was actually, about three years ago, maybe four years ago, a front-page story in the *Chicago Sun-Times*—we had this kid shot. [He] is lying on the ground, and the detective is . . . talking to him . . . and it's his last, dying statement . . . and the detectives asked him, "You know who just shot you—tell us who did it." [He said,] "I'm not telling you anything." To put it mildly—his last breath.[1]

Wysinger has seen whole neighborhoods "clam up" like an oyster rather than reveal who just committed a crime—even if it was against a neighborhood resident. Reporters, too, often encounter the same obstinate treatment when they knock on doors hoping a family member will talk. When police officers canvass a neighborhood, knocking on doors trying to learn who fired the shots that killed a teen riding a bike or an innocent child or that hit a pregnant resident walking down the street, they get nowhere. People who live outside the danger zones don't understand a culture or value system that encourages potential victims to ignore the offers of help. Wysinger understands:

> It's . . . a culmination of things. A fear factor—the mistrust and distrust of the police. And you can actually not be fearful for your-

self . . . but, if you live in some of these communities, even if you can take care of yourself, you have family members—and they may be vulnerable to the gangs. They have to ride the bus back and forth and catch the trains and walk through these neighborhoods. So, that's probably one of the biggest things. [Residents think] if I step up [and talk] as an individual, what happens to my family? Because, they're going to get painted with the same broad "snitch" brush that I'm going to get painted with. So, there's a lot of things that you have to consider.

The Chicago police are considered the good guys. Members of various street gangs are called the bad guys, even by themselves. The two sides are in a committed battle that the police seem to be winning—but not without vital costs in human lives. And other times when the body count is high, it is apparent that the cops are losing the fight.

The Monday after Palm Sunday, April 2014, Father Michael Pfleger, the outspoken activist priest mentioned earlier, was on almost all of the television newscasts in Chicago. Pfleger had blasted the media with several stinging blurbs he had posted on Twitter. Just days before, a white supremacist in Overland, Kansas, had killed three people, sparking a national outrage. Pfleger posted the following on Facebook:

I'm a bit concerned and confused . . . 3 people in Kansas are killed in a tragic shooting and it becomes World News and gets a statement from the White House . . . more than 36 shot and 4 Killed in Chicago in the Bloodiest weekend of the year . . . and its pg 17 of the Sun Times [daily newspaper] and seemingly not important to the Nation! WOW, I guess that's the accepted norm for Chicago . . . and the value of Black and Hispanic life . . . Wake up Brothers, Stop this Madness. You must Value yourself and love yourself more . . . Cause obviously the rest of the Nation doesn't give a

> Damn if you kill yourselves off . . . and the privatized prisons will make a ton of money off you![2]

Father Pfleger is a savvy media scholar, as well. But what he fails to realize is that assignment editors and producers won't react to a bloody weekend in Chicago as he would like for them to respond, because they are jaded and exhausted from covering the same types of senseless shootings and mayhem. And not surprisingly, since the thirty-six victims were in different parts of town and suffered their injuries in separate actions, the cases only received casual mention. It's all about perception. If thirty-six people had been shot in a ritzy, tree-lined North Shore Chicago suburb, we'd still be doing that story, years later; it just wouldn't die. But when, over a bloody weekend, thirty-six citizens of poor neighborhoods in Chicago are shot, the following Monday news reporters relate the grisly total, shove a microphone in the face of the police superintendent, and ask "why" and "how." They play the response from the top cop and then move on to another story. But when the media begins to play up a case or make high crime the "flavor of the month," police begin to feel the pressure. Al Wysinger says the more communities hear from news reports about murders, the more they think "that could've been my son— that could've been my daughter," and they're more likely to speak with police or reporters.[3]

COMPUTERIZED CRIME FIGHTING

But murder stories in high-crime neighborhoods will continue to only receive marginal coverage because of a simple perception: these are bad guys killing bad guys . . . and who cares? That misguided perception is widely held, especially in neighborhoods where violence is low. But the type of crime caused by drug traffic is insidious and creeps into upscale neighborhoods when suburban kids support their drug habits by slipping into the inner city to buy their narcotics. Sooner or later the thug life will inch its way into middle- and upper-class neighborhoods. Former Chicago police superintendent Garry McCarthy knows that and is trying to be creative in his law enforcement tactics, hoping to outfox the street gangs:

> I think we're doing a lot better . . . and we're putting officers back on the beats. Those officers are accountable for what goes on in the beats and they get to know the good people from the bad people so we don't just stop everybody—we stopped the right people because they know who the criminals are.[4]

It's not a novel approach; McCarthy is using a computerized system that was instituted by William Bratton, the top cop in Boston and commissioner of the NYPD. Called the CompStat System, this data-driven method of tracking crime tries to predict where the next infraction will occur before it happens. It aims to cut crime in so-called "hot areas" around the city. An article in *Chicago* magazine looked at the system and how it works. The system gathers information on criminal activity and generates a report showing crime statistics for every district. The statistics help make officers in those districts responsible. "I got to show my wares at CompStat," McCarthy said, after his positive results. "And, quite frankly, I did very well."[5]

McCarthy says that much of his policing philosophy grew out of Bratton's approach, which worked so well that the city's subsequent police chiefs rode it to historic drops in crime. Simply put, Bratton did three things: First, he implemented CompStat. Second, he acted on the "broken windows" theory; that is, he instructed cops to crack down on minor offenses—curfew violations, loud music, graffiti, public intoxication, and so on—because any bad deed could lead to more serious criminal behavior. Third, he collapsed the layers of bureaucracy, eliminating middle managers and emphasizing the job of the beat cop. "It has to do with accountability," explains McCarthy.

"If [officers] don't have a beat, if they're not accountable for any-thing, all they're doing is going from job to job."[6]

But while the CompStat system may work well to reduce some crimes, it seems to have little effect on street gang shootings—crimes that are, many times, based on revenge or a senseless craving for status, a yearning for "street cred" that defies logic and rational explanation. So the bad guys continue to step out of alleys, armed with high-powered assault rifles, and begin shooting into groups of the "others": people who live on another gang turf. It doesn't matter who catches the bullet—a mother, a baby, a grandfather, or a member of a rival faction.

The malevolent and wanton manner with which the shooters discharge their weapons shows that they really don't care that they have taken an innocent life. Not until they are caught and find them-selves behind bars do they stop long enough to consider just how stupid they are acting. Psychiatrist Carl Bell asserts that some of this behavior is due to pregnant mothers' drinking habits during early stages of pregnancy . . . and more sadly and damaging, for some, throughout gestation:

> Probably 75, 85 percent of the women who are using crack were abused as children—before they were even old enough to know what crack was. Crack, though, is not the major problem for the intellectual problems—it's alcohol. And if you go into special edu-cation in schools and you look at the seven-year-olds—because that's where it shows up—a lot of that stuff is fetal alcohol . . . maybe half of the children in special ed.[7]

Dr. Bell says these inordinately high numbers help explain why we see so many instances of kids who act in such a cold-blooded manner, snuffing out a human life as easily as swatting a fly:

> There's one study in Canada where they have Native American people that showed that nineteen out of twenty children in a deten-

tion center had fetal alcohol exposure, because [the authorities] are more aware of it than we are. And when you go to Child Protective Services you see a lot of parents who had fetal alcohol exposure and children who had fetal alcohol exposure. So that's a problem. The problem is that neuroscience, neuropsychiatry has not been humane enough or public health–conscious enough to be able to come up with a brain-imaging test to solidly identify [the syndrome] objectively.

That helps to explain some of the violence, but unless the public learns about statistics like those given by Dr. Bell the perception will remain that the shooters are merely "bad guys," the outcasts, to be ignored and ostracized. But until reporters are able to do more than just stand in front of yellow police tape reciting statistics, the deeper subject matter of what is causing the violence will never be reported. And when editors don't call for more in-depth looks at theory, preferring instead quick ninety-second stories, then the message will continue to be "style over substance."

Another approach the media might take is to look at the issues in a more in-depth fashion. Ava Thompson Greenwell aims to help her students at the Medill School of Journalism see that it's "how" they cover stories in high-crime areas that makes a difference:

> And, so, they may do a quick reader or a v/o [voice-over] on those murders on the West Side, because, again, that's what happens on the West Side. But, have they ever been to the West Side? They don't know anybody on the West Side, and so they don't have any connection to the West Side. So Hinsdale, a suburban area, [will] say, "I can relate to that."[8]

Meanwhile, heroin addiction has already begun to spread into white suburbs. States like Maine and Ohio are calling it an epidemic.[9] Families who fled the violence of the inner city are now discovering that their children are shooting up heroin and smoking crack in alarming numbers. And now programs like ABC's *20/20* and CBS's *60 Minutes* are devoting huge segments of their shows to the issue of heroin addiction in the suburbs. The focus is on treatment and intervention. But years ago when narcotics in black neighborhoods were seen as a problem, the government instituted the War on Drugs, locking up offenders—some for life sentences. It should be embarrassing to the executive producers of these shows that they have the "moxie" to now call heroin a scourge when it has been a menace in minority neighborhoods for decades. News directors have the responsibility to call their producers on the carpet when obvious prejudicial reporting occurs. If they don't, they risk making their stations look foolish because viewers are not dumb. They know the drug problem flowed through minority communities for years, ruining families while authorities incarcerated thousands of young men.

EX-OFFENDERS ARE GETTING A SECOND CHANCE AT LIFE

Over the years I've received hundreds of letters from prisoners, some claiming their innocence and others expressing their sorrow for acting in such a rabid manner before they were sentenced. But by then it was too late: their lives and those of the families of the victims had been destroyed by the impulsive action of pointing a firearm and not knowing what was on the other side. The prisoners just pulled the trigger and let the bullets fly.

So journalists who have been covering this kind of heinous behavior, year after year, become hardened and impenitent toward bad guys. They unapologetically disregard covering their dirty deeds unless the crimes are so shocking that there is no way to overlook them.

The police superintendent keeps reminding citizens that fighting crime is every person's responsibility. And while crime statistics were dropping in the city in 2015, 2016 was one of the most violent years in recent history. Over seven hundred murders have been committed, and by the end of the year Chicago could reach almost eight hundred.[10] Police say a culture of "not being a snitch" hampers their efforts to catch criminals.[11] Wysinger says,

> It's a culture, and it does kind of defeat some of the things that we have to do, but we have to step back several decades and actually ask ourselves what the reasons [are for] the communities [to be] so distrustful of law enforcement and start from there. There are some good examples and some very good reasons why people in certain communities just don't embrace and trust the police.[12]

Wysinger understands that distrust of police, in certain neighborhoods, is natural—that decades of police abuse and misconduct have led to the fears and apprehensions that many residents have, why people refuse to pick up a phone and call to report on their neighbors. "[I]t's going to take a concerted effort," Wysinger says of mending the bridge between the community and the police, "and unless we get the community to trust us—to come from behind the doors and actually start telling on some of the individuals who are committing these crimes—we're going to continue to see this violence perpetuate."[13]

Former Illinois governor Pat Quinn has taken steps to try and reduce recidivism. In August 2013, Quinn signed a few pieces of legislation that he says will give ex-offenders a second chance at employment and a productive life. The legislation provides additional options in sentencing nonviolent offenders, and one bill allows for the removal of a nonviolent conviction from an offender's record after two years, or more, of probation. The new laws were to begin January 1, 2014.[14]

Without jobs, many of the ex-offenders are doomed to head back to prison because they will do whatever it takes to get their hands on some money. Therefore, another bill helps employers by increasing their income tax credit from $600 to $1,500 for each employee if they provide a job to an ex-offender with the appropriate skill sets.[15]

Yet there has to be a balanced approach in how criminals are treated: Try to rehabilitate them if possible so they can become productive citizens. But don't protect their identities if they stray and commit crimes. Then they must live out that old axiom, "if you do the crime you got to do the time."

Father Pfleger preaches the same mantra—"Don't protect the criminals."[16] His parish is at ground zero. Violent crime surrounds his church, but his parishioners do report wrongdoing. They are not afraid to stand up to the thugs who are, after all, the children of some absentee parent.

People who are critical of Father Pfleger should drive to his church in Chicago and take a look at what he has built. The immediate area surrounding his parish is a flourishing oasis in the otherwise bleak, worn-out, scary, and crime-ridden Auburn Gresham neighborhood. Street gangs are everywhere; drug sales are booming in something akin to an open-air bazaar. But at St. Sabina Catholic Church no litter blows about the sidewalks, playground equipment is clean and in good working order, and there is a welcoming brightness—a radiance that revitalizes this part of the forsaken, mournful community.

As you drive through the neighborhood surrounding St. Sabina, everything looks wretched—no one smiles, no children are playing, trash fills the gutters and vacant lots, no one is watering the grass, and there are no flowers. You won't have any trouble seeing thugs standing watch on street corners. The "lookouts" use hand signals to pass the word ahead—with lightning speed—that potential drug buyers are approaching or cops are on the way.

The only residents who do venture out are elderly people, slowly making their way down the shattered sidewalks, past boarded-up storefronts. They are ignored by the young, predatory thugs because the hunched-over seniors have nothing worth stealing. Even so, on days when Social Security checks need to be cashed, the elderly try to catch a ride to the currency exchange with a relative or neighbor. After cashing their meager checks, they take refuge once again inside their homes. Pfleger is quick to rant on Facebook and Twitter, saying things about conditions in his community that no one else has the guts to say:

> They say they can't even put a figure on the money that our Government and others around the World have spent and are spending trying to find the missing plane (Malaysian Flt. 370). . . . [A]nd as of now the US has spent well over a Billion in the Ukraine but there is STILL no money for Education, Jobs, Economic Development in the Urban Community, After School programs and Violence Prevention. . . . Now we're told The Chicago Police Department lied about numbers of Shootings . . . and BTW when they tell us that America's Unemployment is 6.7% It must mean Englewood, Auburn Gresham, Lawndale are not part of America. . . . My Question is WHEN ARE WE GOING TO SAY ENOUGH???????[17]

DO THE BAD GUYS DESERVE OUR HELP?

As a minister, Pfleger does not bite his tongue when he "calls out" government leaders, local politicians, or anyone who could possibly help curb the violence that continues to claim lives of young African American men in his community. I asked him once if he had been approached by big-money individuals who had hoped to make financial donations to him (bribes) in an effort to secure his silence—especially on issues that might squelch an opportunity for the donor to make even more money. Pfleger said, "I tell them I've been bought off once, by Jesus. So, I can't be bought anymore."[18]

When he complains that not enough resources are being thrown at the crime problem he is constantly combating, deep down inside, he knows why. The gang members are considered bad guys who are killing other bad guys. And no one really cares or wants to step in and stop the madness. Pfleger told me during an interview that he understood why some young men joined gangs. He didn't condone it but understood:

> People are getting affiliated [joining gangs] just because they live in a certain area. That doesn't mean that they hang with the gang— do with the gang. You cannot live in certain areas of the city, and not be connected to or affiliated with the [street gangs]. These are still necessary to live and go back and forth every night. So we are connected. We are affiliated. But, does that mean your life is not valuable? Your life is not important because you're gang affiliated or a gangbanger?[19]

It's the different classes of people who seem to receive the different levels of media attention. Sometimes all the special elements are present that make a story zing to the top of the interest scale. Hadiya Pendleton's story, which was sensationalized like few other murders, continues to be followed as each anniversary of her death is recognized. But her case is not without equivalent. Many murder cases rivet the public's attention like few others.

Seven years before Hadiya Pendleton, Starkesia Reed, a fourteen-year-old honor student at Harper High School in Chicago's Englewood neighborhood, was shot and killed by random gunfire in 2006.[20] It was shortly before eight o'clock in the morning when Starkesia went to the window to look down the street for her friends. A bullet from a high-powered assault rifle, fired almost a block away, struck her in the head, killing her instantly. Her death became headline news.

Then, a little more than a week later, ten-year-old Siretha White was killed by a stray bullet just two days before her eleventh birthday. White had gone to a surprise birthday party for her cousin without realizing the festivities would be for her as well.[21]

But in the middle of the celebration gunfire erupted outside her aunt's Englewood home, and the awful sound of shattering glass frightened the youngsters. Siretha had been fatally shot in the head by a bullet that had pierced the front window. Siretha's mother told me that the shock and pain of losing a daughter ultimately killed her husband, the child's father:

[A]fter he found out that our daughter got killed . . . he went down. He went into intensive care, and he never recovered. So, I was trying to wait for him to help me put our daughter away, but he never came back—he went straight downhill. Then, when we went to the burial for my daughter, the hospital called. I never got to see my daughter go in down to the ground, because the hospital called and they rushed me [there]. And, as I was walking through the door, he raised up and looked at me and smiled and laid back down and went to rest.[22]

In one week, Siretha Woods, a mother and wife, lost two family members: a daughter from a stray bullet and the girl's father, who died from a broken heart. A family was shattered and in wretched misery all because an idiot with a grudge fired a rifle with wanton disregard for who would die that day—seemingly, it didn't matter.

How did it happen that two innocent children, both with bright futures, were inside a home doing kid things when they were viciously struck down in an unbelievably cruel fashion? It baffles the imagination and seems, to me, unthinkable that something so horrible could happen—with such anticipated regularity—while we are not in a state of war. Former Chicago police superintendent Garry McCarthy says police are slowly making a dent in the high-crime numbers.

"Progress is progress," McCarthy explains, "and the fact is we talk about progress and not success, in this we've been talking about. We have systems in place that address it. It's a step-by-step, day-by-day grind. . . . Unfortunately we can do everything right sometimes and it still ends up with people getting shot."[23]

But stories are seldom told about police efforts in trying new programs or about neighborhood do-gooders who risk their lives in order to make the neighborhood safer. Television news organizations usually reserve the "in-depth stories" for ratings months or the once-in-a-while cover stories that allow reporters to spend three or four minutes to devote to a subject that normally gets one minute and twenty seconds. Weekend news producer Sean Leidigh would like to see more attention given to thoughtful stories:

> I remember we did a story about a little girl who got shot, and it was one of those—we've had a few of those a summer—where a little kid is in the wrong place at the wrong time and got shot. And really the details of this were about fifteen seconds—a little girl sitting outside with her parents, and [she] got a bullet by someone who may not have aimed at her. But the story we ended up telling was [about] her grandmother, who went about the state [speaking about the shooting]. That was the important part of the story, and I don't think we do enough of that. We don't find the stories that stick with people as opposed to just another murder—another sexual assault.[24]

INTENSE NEWS COVERAGE MAKES GANG LEADERS SWEAT

Here is some information you won't hear anywhere else. Even though it is the gang members who are shooting and, for the most part, getting shot, when a murder becomes sensationalized and blows up in the media, gang leaders hate it. As was mentioned in an earlier chapter, high-profile cases draw the ire of the mayor and other city officials. And when television stations and newspapers are hammering away at a single homicide, there is only one thing the gang leaders can do—give up the shooter. Someone will "drop a dime."[25]

The leaders won't admit this to their sycophantic underlings, but with police swarming all over the neighborhood looking for clues to help solve the murder, the gangs can't make any money selling drugs. The sustained high-impact nature of the story continues to draw reporters and camera crews back to the scene, with minicam trucks rolling all through the neighborhood. This continues to keep the crime in the consciousness of the public and makes the story even bigger, causing more pressure to come from the top of the pecking order. With all this attention, gang leaders will do whatever it takes to try and have things return to normal. Somebody's girlfriend will make an anonymous call to police headquarters alerting officers to the whereabouts of the shooter: so much for "one love." Furthermore, any other illicit activity the bad guys were involved in would also come to a screeching halt because of the mounting pressure to solve the crime.

Bad guys getting killed is often thought of by the public as thugs "getting what they deserve." Yet the killers are so pervasive that not all the culprits are males. Once in a while there is an "Annie Oakley"—a modern-day gunslinger who defies all the conventions of gender and who seems to worship the "thug life" to such an extent that her impermanence is almost guaranteed. Take the case of Gakirah Barnes, a five-foot-three, 128-pound seventeen-year-old girl who became a reputed female gang assassin. Barnes became the subject of a feature article in the *Chicago Sun-Times*, which chronicled her short life as a "shooter," someone police referred to as a gang assassin.[26]

The sorrowful story of Gakirah Barnes won't leave many people shedding tears for her. And if she did kill as many as fifteen rival gang members, she *is* an example of bad guys killing bad guys, one less cold-blooded, psychopathic villain for the rest of us to be concerned about.

But not all murders receive headline treatment, and the relatives of those victims and the family members of the shooters are all left to wonder in grief, "Why didn't the murder of my son or daughter or cousin ever make the news?" The silence of the media only adds to the anguish and sorrow for the innocent surviving family members who have done nothing wrong. For the relatives of the gunman (or woman), their only unfortunate circumstance was to have been born into a family with an idiotic next of kin.

Chapter Seven

THE PHANTOM AUDIENCE IN US ALL

Most street reporters I know, and work with almost daily, rarely think specifically about the audience or viewers they are informing. So it could be argued that they do not know their audience. That is the way it has been for decades. But journalists today in the newly created positions of web producers do know their audience. In fact, they know very well who is clicking on the television station website. If you talk to Anna Roberts, online news producer at WGN-TV.com and CLTV.com, you learn that this neophyte position packs a lot of influence with station bosses who want to know which stories are popular, at the moment, on the site:

> We have a software system that shows [relatively] up-to-the-minute results of what's hot on the site. Now we use "day-to-day" and month's end reports, as far as what went well and what people were looking at and that kind of thing. . . .
>
> [We look at] stats . . . the metrics—that's what we call them. Not really so much to determine the programming for the home page or anything like that—we don't want that to drive what we are trying. It's always a toss-up. We'll look at video—a cat playing a piano, the mayor's putting out new parking meter rules—that's important too . . . or pension reform, which is not a very . . . click-able topic but important to the state. So, that cat playing the piano is getting way more hits. . . . So—we have flexibility in our site as to what we highlight—in different things all at the same time.[1]

These types of journalistic decisions are new. The station web page is only a few years old, and the technology governing how web producers evaluate the wishes of web surfers who stop by the site is also relatively new.

This new Internet paradigm has created its own set of ethical issues. If, as a journalist, you know that you have a responsibility to inform the viewers about the complicated issue of choosing health-care alternatives, but at the same time you know the story of a dancing polar bear will skyrocket, do you place the healthcare story behind the polar bear?

Based on this kind of data, earlier scholars concluded that audience imagery, which years ago could not be clearly determined with such accuracy, wasn't important in the building of news. Yet audience image *is* important. And the picture of the audience is principally bound up in product image, and it was not easily clarified by the journalist until the last five or six years. In 2017, producers have an almost exact understanding of who is clicking on to the web to view news stories.

WGN-TV web producer Elyse Russo says,

> [W]e can also see how many unique visits we have had to the website. If [people] click through the story, we can see how many of them have watched that video that we've attached to the story, so that's pretty cool. . . .
>
> When I look at it—I'm actually going through the month right now and seeing which stories had the most views, which videos had the most views—I like to share that with the team so they know which ones are doing the best.[2]

Everette Dennis in his book *Reshaping the Media* is quite right when he contends that responses by journalists to questions about audience are "incredibly unscientific."[3] By that he means they are not tied to findings from well-designed social research. Still, editors and producers do have an understanding of their audience, stemming from their work in producing news stories. But during the heat of a breaking story, most assignment editors say audience is the last thing on their minds.

Assignment editor Pat Curry says, "When I sit up here and I hear about a shooting, I'm not thinking about the audience; I'm thinking about that story—is it a story there? I mean, you have to come back with something. . . . And it also depends on what kind of resources we send."[4]

Each day as journalists begin their shifts, whether in the morning ("day side") or the afternoon ("night side"), they attend a meeting to go over the events of the day. These editorial meetings allow journalists to have a greater understanding of what has already been covered that day and what is scheduled for later newscasts.

During these meetings an open discussion is held so that producers, reporters, assignment editors, writers, and anyone who will be a part of the news production process is on the same page. At this time, reporters get their assignments and the executive producer gives an indication as to which stories will be stacked more prominently in the show. Of course, all of this is subject to change. If a breaking story occurs, producers will "blow up" the show in order to rearrange all of the content in the newscast: some stories will need to be dropped because of time; others will be pushed up or down in the show or moved from one segment to another. Depending on the magnitude of the breaking news, the entire remainder of the show could be devoted to the story (examples are plane crashes, multiple murder victims, earthquakes, or major disasters).

What news workers see as their primary task is creating product: individual news stories or the newscast as a whole. If the primary focus of the journalist is gathering materials for constructing stories, it is a mistake not to look at the influence of the audience on how the journalist constructs his or her story. But since journalists are primarily concerned with creating the news product, most of the time, they may not be able to cohesively describe their understandings of their audience, or they may not even care.

But each story calls for a different approach. For example, if a reporter was covering a story about mold and mildew being found in a middle school, she would know going out the door that a story like this would take more time to tell than a murder story. The mildew story would require a more personal approach—finding a parent who has children in the school and getting his or her reaction to the discovery. Instead of only talking to the principal or superintendent, the reporter would try talking to the CEO of the abatement company that would be cleaning the school or a local scientist who could describe the type of mold found and whether it would pose a danger to students.

If this were a suburban school in an adjoining county, the producer would begin to sweat, fearing that the reporter might not make the deadline because of travel time or the reporter would have a weak story because there wasn't sufficient time to develop all the elements in the story.

On the other hand, if a reporter was rushed out the door to cover a murder story located in the same suburb as the school with mold, once he arrived in the neighborhood the crew could set up, begin shooting video of the scene (at the least yellow police tape and flashing blue lights), and beam back shots of the neighborhood. The reporter could grab a neighbor or a "kid on a bike" and ask an inane question, such as, "What do you know about the people who live in that house?" In no time the reporter at the murder scene would have produced a two-minute story, a story that didn't supply very much information but that looked flashy and allowed the anchors to seem anxious and concerned. And that would also allay some of the producer's fears about missing "slot" or a deadline.

The reporter at the school might not have more than a voice-over and pictures of the school with a sign in the door saying, "Closed until

Further Notice." And while the mildew story could have serious consequences for hundreds of students, the story might be pushed down in the show or dropped altogether, if the reporter at the murder story found an interesting interview or had shots of the family screaming and crying . . . or of a suspect being marched away in handcuffs.

Decisions like the ones above are made every day. And at the root of each decision is the producer's gut feeling that the audience is more interested in one story over another.

Understanding the makeup of different locales is important in deciding which stories to cover. Just because a crime occurred in a suburb might be reason enough to go there. Assignment editors know which parts of their viewing area are typically known for different things. But other times without sufficient information, assignment editors dispatch reporters who go into an area blind and have to start from scratch. Assignment editor Pat Curry says,

> [S]ometimes you just can't tell. We had a story last week where we knew something violent had occurred inside a house—it was in Addison, a suburb—and crime when it happens in the suburbs may be a story because it happened in the suburbs. You know some suburbs are known to be more prone to violence than others. If there is a crime in Winnetka I would say Bob's interview is being cut off [if I was the reporter on another assignment] because we've got to go to Winnetka, because [crime] doesn't happen in Winnetka . . . and so when it does—there is something up with that and we need to check it out.[5]

These types of choices are made at each station in the same market. If viewers began to switch stations and surf around the dial at the beginning of the hour, most of the time all stations would be broadcasting the same story. There is no collusion or conspiracy among producers. They don't call each other and say, "What's your lead?" Most of the time the stories themselves dictate how and where, in the show, they will be placed. On busy news days when a lot is going on, the lead story will more than likely be the same at each station. But on slow news days when assignment editors have to be creative and hunt for stories to cover, chances are the lead stories will be different at each station. And each producer will have a reason for going with one story over another. Even news director Jennifer Lyons is sometimes amazed when she watches, in the control room, three or four television sets simultaneously:

> What amazes me as a producer . . . is to have all the networks up on the air and they are all broadcasting [the same story]—you go in with a list of stories and you decide, okay we're going to do this child shot, we're going to do this garbage collection story, we're going to do this and use it, and you watch every single other network. How does it happen [that] every single station is on the same exact story? There might be a little story in between that's different, but [they're] literally stacked the same way—and it is—it's the news-room mentality. It's been what producers think and the assignment editors say when selling the story . . . and all of a sudden, we're all on the same story and we're all telling virtually the same story.[6]

It is by examining news executives' understanding of the products they produce that one learns how different perceptions of the audience do impact news construction. Simple models of communication imply that the extent to which the audience supplies input into the journalistic product produces a direct relationship between audience and journalist. E-mail from the audience is carefully screened, and each piece is read. It's true that the squeaky wheel does get the oil. Viewers who call television stations do have an influence on what journalists understand about the stories they put on TV. When I speak to groups, I always tell them, to their surprise, just how much influence they have just by taking the time to write a news director or station manager.

THE PHANTOM AUDIENCE IN US ALL

The journalist learns about the audience, either directly from the audience member (phone calls, e-mails, letters to the editor, and talk on the street) or from within the news organization (which has presumably engaged in formal audience analyses ratings, readership studies, and focus groups). Those are indeed a part of the dynamic of story construction . . . but so, too, are the implicit understandings that grow out of working in news day after day.

Today, journalists who file stories that end up on the web have the opportunity to read the comment section to judge audience reaction to the story. WGN-TV/CLTV web producer Anna Roberts says the comments sometimes can be offensive. "[T]hey can get nasty and awful," Roberts explains. "I don't like or prefer to read them because it makes me so sad about humanity. . . . People on news sites are more interested to comment and share their feelings, blame whoever, use derogatory names, and stuff like that."[7]

Journalists may be vague in their descriptions and imagery of their audience, and that is to be expected, again, because journalists by and large function to create news, which is a product. On a day-to-day basis, the journalist typically has little time to seriously ponder how well she is communicating with an audience member. Viewers might be envisioned in the classic basic communication model: the source preparing a message for a receiver to transmit over a channel and then further reacting to feedback. Therefore, journalists do not readily voice a formal theory or detailed information about their audience. Over the years I have observed arguments between assignment editors—even screaming and hollering—as they disagree on how to cover a story or situation. Assignment editor Chris Neale notes,

> It's all about gut—Kelly's got a gut feeling, and I've got a gut feeling, and this [story] is a big one, and it might catch her attention differently than it does mine. And maybe she talked to somebody and I didn't, so she's got to convince me—just like I had to convince them—that I think this is a good one. Things that stand

out are age, so children obviously are [a priority]. If someone is fifty to sixty . . . anybody over seventy who was a victim of crime, bears looking more closely at. The ones that probably get the least amount of attention are eighteen to twenty-four.[8]

Both implicit and explicit understandings of the audience and its influence are an important consideration in the construction of news and how decisions are made as to which stories to cover. There is no formal theory of audience supporting the construction of news texts, but understandings of audience developed through a variety of journalistic activities do make their impact on the news.

Understandings about the audience are embedded, for example, in the technology that news organizations acquire. The notion that audiences want fast-paced, instantaneous information will lead a television station to focus on purchasing live-broadcast equipment. And since murders are the types of stories that fit well within a "breaking news" format, they become easy-access tools for loading up the first segment of a newscast.

CRANKING OUT THE NEWS

Journalists often talk about their work in language akin to a "manu-facturing" mode. For example, Chris Neale described his duties as becoming routine. He has to remind himself to remember that he's dealing with human subjects:

> What we're dealing with are human beings, and every time you hear about a shooting, a murder, a homicide, it means someone has lost a loved one. And we tend to forget about that sometimes—it's just another person or another story to us, which is terrible. . . . [Y]ou do get desensitized to it. And, if [it] happened in a certain neighbor-hood—it's not really news, because it happened there . . . because it's been an ongoing problem for twenty-some years, at least.[9]

By this, the assignment editor suggests that much of his work is performed quickly and relatively efficiently, with each employee completing his or her assigned tasks, as in an assembly line. Similarly, retired WGN news director Greg Caputo remembers a time, decades ago, when there were no "live shots" in a newscast. Since then there have been many important changes in the delivery of news. "[There] have been several," Caputo says. "The one that had already set itself up, but was growing, when I first became a news director, was live TV. It's hard to remember."[10]

Live shots are so routine today that producers often send reporters back out to the scene of an earlier event, during the show, even though nothing is going on there. The police tape has been removed, and life has returned to normal. But reporters are still sent back to recount what happened earlier in the day. (This is happening less today than a couple of years ago because some of the neighborhoods at night—and even during the day—are just too dangerous. Flashy live trucks during the day and well-lit reporters after dark can be easy targets for gang members who shoot first and think later.) Even so, viewers have become savvier and see through bogus attempts to sensationalize a story by returning to the scene when there is no reason to be there.

Caputo thinks "truth in reporting" is becoming more necessary as viewers have access to the same tools that are used by journalists. He believes social media has changed how news is viewed. "People are getting their news from Twitter," Caputo says. "I get a tweet, and I follow NBC News or follow ABC News or I follow the Drudge Report or whatever I follow, and that becomes the Gospel. . . . And I think over [this] period of time, too, newscasts, TV news stories, [along with] the attention span of viewers seem to demand a quicker broadcast with more . . . bell ringers in it, to grab and hold someone's attention."[11]

Caputo realizes that stories are a commodity of the trade. His language, "more bell ringers in it, to grab and hold someone's attention," connotes a manufacturing mentality. Also deadline pressure forces the journalist to narrow his focus to the immediate job at hand, "cranking out" the news story. But as more stories are produced day in and day out, the regularity forces some assignment editors to rely on instincts. Natalie Costa is also an attorney who worked the desk while she was in law school:

> It's a combination of a couple of things . . . I just have been doing this so long that a lot of it becomes mechanical. You just go by your news judgment, and it becomes refined over time, and things you may not have thought of as being big ten years ago—you evolve from that point. So that's part of it. . . . Visually, I don't think about the viewers. I think about [the fact that] we've seen it all; honestly, we've seen it all. So, a lot of it goes based on gut. You hear something, you go "Oh my God." You just haven't seen that before in your life. You're going to [assign a crew] because you know it's a big deal; you haven't even heard of that before.[12]

Over and over, journalists keep saying that there is something innate that helps them make decisions—a "nose for news" that guides them and helps them make good, solid decisions. But isn't that the case in every profession? Don't stockbrokers read the market and react to conditions that prompt them to buy or sell? Don't doctors see a patient come into the emergency room and make snap judgments based on a few outward signs and symptoms? And don't plumbers and police officers and firefighters make snap decisions—critical calls—that are based on a few assumptions and a lot of intuition? Of course they all do. But the difference is that the decisions made by journalists are eventually evaluated by the public. Often hundreds, thousands, or even millions of viewers or readers receive their information based on journalists' judgments. And sometimes public policy can be swayed by what journalists report. That's seldom the case when a doctor decides if a patient has appendicitis or a bad case of gas.

Most of the time, seasoned assignment editors and producers are correct. The decisions they make turn out to be good news choices. I'll never forget a story I covered in January 1988. This was a particularly harsh winter in Chicago with subzero temperatures that lingered for days. And when the thermometer did inch its way up a bit, the biting cold still remained in the single digits or lower teens.

With these frigid conditions in mind, I was assigned a story that took me and my cameraman, Richard "Ike" Isaac, to Gary, Indiana—about forty minutes from Chicago. The assignment desk had received a tip from a carpenter for a board-up service (companies that place sheets of plywood over windows and doors to secure abandoned buildings), saying that he'd discovered a small child in the freezing attic of an uninhabited house. The caller said the girl had cried out to him when he began hammering to cover up the tiny upstairs window. He looked inside and saw the girl on the floor in a barren, trash-filled room with McDonald's papers and cartons strewn about.

The sobbing, shivering child told the worker that she couldn't stand up, that her feet were hurting too much and that she was very cold. The worker asked the girl through the window if she was alone. She said her mother sometimes came by to bring her food but that she hadn't seen her in a few days. Horrified, the worker called the Gary Police Department and then called our television station.

By the time Ike and I arrived at the location of the abandoned house, the deserted child, the worker (who didn't want to go on camera, anyway), and everyone from the police and social welfare department had left. We headed to the Gary Police Department to talk to someone who could give us details about this incident. A sergeant we interviewed told us in detail about the case. He said the girl's name was Darlwin Carlisle; she was nine years old.

There were conflicting reports about how long the girl and her mother had lived in the house. Lake County state's attorney Jack Craw-ford said Darlwin Carlisle told authorities her mother, Darlwin Britt, twenty-four, "kept telling her she would bring food and water, but never did." After being discovered and taken to a children's hospital, doctors were forced to amputate Darlwin's legs just below her knees.[13]

Covering this story, Ike and I were in tears. Hearing the suffering child had lost both legs was gut-wrenching. Even so, we continued to cover the saga of Darlwin day after day.

We went to her school and learned that for many years the mother had been destitute but still had continued to send Darlwin to school in clean and neat dresses. The child was well liked and was a good student. But something awful, something terrible had happened to her mother to make her so callous and thoughtless— leaving the young girl alone in deadly, subfreezing temperatures day after day with little or no food and hardly any clothing. How could a mother do this to her child—how could any parent do such a thing?

We learned that the mother had become strung out on drugs and had undergone a horrible transformation from a loving, caring mother to a drug fiend. Everyone wanted to see what this mother, now called a monster, looked like. So Ike and I staked out the judicial center after one of her court appearances. We waited for the state police car to drive her out of the court building and return her to jail.

Instead of Ike driving, I took the wheel and put Ike in the shotgun seat with his camera. As the police left we followed them, at first unnoticed, but we were soon recognized as press. The cops sped off with us behind them. Imagine, we were pursuing the cops, and they led us on quite a chase. But once we pulled onto the expressway, we had him. Even though the sheriff had his lights flashing and siren blasting, I pulled alongside. Ike began rolling and got video of Darlwin Britt, the mother, sitting in the back seat. With her hands cuffed behind her back, she couldn't cover her face, so Ike had a pretty good shot. The sheriff kept his speed at the limit long enough for us to get good shots, and then he looked at us, smiled, and sped off, leaving us in his dust.

The innocuous tip of a child in an attic turned out to be a much talked about story that drew the attention of nearly everyone in Chicago. Darlwin's story is also one I will never forget. For almost thirty years I have thought of her often. A quick gut decision by the assignment editor had turned out to be good judgment. I followed the story, even on my days off, to learn what was going on in the child's life. I remember when Darlwin walked out of the hospital three months later. Doctors said she had most of her abilities and all the energy of a cheerful youngster.

Darlwin had been fitted with artificial limbs. She limped very slightly but smiled and held two dolls when she walked down the front steps of La Rabida Children's Hospital.

IS IT DOABLE?

Another expression used by journalists to characterize news is whether it's "doable." To be accomplished, news has to be doable. For WGN assignment editor Natalie Costa, that means a potential story that won't take too long to put together so it will be ready for the next newscast. "Sometimes," Costa says, "you'd have a little kid drown . . . far away—you can't go because you just don't have some-body to take a chance and go to drive two hours and hope that it's really a story."[14]

Deadline pressures force journalists to narrow their focus to the immediate job at hand: cranking out the news story. Many producers try to have so-called "evergreen" (canned) stories in the files that can be pulled out at the last minute and put in the show, if it is a slow news day or if a major story falls apart.

Planned news stories are a major part of the business of producing news. Planned stories are thought of in advance and produced when the organization deems it appropriate. Most of the time these stories or "specials" are centered around "sweeps" or ratings months, four times a year when key viewer analysis is taken and advertising rates are set, based on those aggregate numbers. News director Jennifer Lyons says the new methods and tools used to track viewers and Internet surfers require an adjustment:

> [E]very time we get new technology, we think, "Oh, man, this is going to be so easy." But, it does take something away from the whole process. . . . It also adds to the process. We get there quicker; we get there faster—get the signal in—usually right away to [the newsroom]. . . . But, there is something about the old journalism with a capital "J" that gets lost. But, that is where the industry is improving. That's where we are right now. But at the same time, the way we used to do it gave us more time . . . for making any sense [of the numbers].[15]

TURNING PLANNED STORIES INTO BREAKING NEWS

Many important discussions focus on readying journalists to carry out their planned activities. The notion that top-story news coverage can be scheduled ahead of time is clearly demonstrated by a station's coverage of local elections.

Television stations go to great lengths to prepare for election coverage. The actual process of getting out information to the viewers about individual candidates actually begins weeks in advance with debate coverage. Candidates are usually assigned to specific reporters who will follow each one and zero in on that candidate's specific platforms.

The advantage of covering one candidate to the end of the campaign gives the reporter an opportunity to get to know the candidate well and understand the fluctuating poll numbers and trends during the campaign. Then on election night the reporter can add gravitas to her reports on why the candidate is doing so well or so poorly. This is a case where planned events become top stories at a later date. But by the time the polls close, the votes have been counted and something unexpected or expected happens: the planned event may now become breaking news. The station interrupts programming with blaring headlines, urgent-sounding jingles, and fast-talking anchors declaring Candidate A to be a winner and Candidate B to be a loser.

Another way a slot in the news show can be filled is with the wait-and-see story. In major cities like Chicago, when reporters do not get assigned stories from the morning editorial meeting, producers may sometimes gamble that something will happen—i.e., a fire, a shooting, a bad accident, or a weather anomaly. This is usually a safe bet. By the time the news program hits the air, something will have happened and the reporter will have rushed to the scene to get the story on the air.

Now, new technology like the Dejero box helps get the story on the air almost instantly. Dejero boxes are the newest toy used by broadcasters to get stories on the air. About the size of two briefcases stacked on top of each other, the Dejero box is an apparatus that uses a series of six cell phone modems inside the box. The modems work in tandem to produce a signal large enough and strong enough to transmit a video signal from the attached camera back to the television station (the same way people send video from cell phone to cell phone, except TV high-definition video requires huge amounts of space or memory).

The box is portable and can be slung over the shoulder or pushed on a tiny hand truck like the ones used to carry bags throughout the airport. The box can be used in many different ways and can be used to broadcast live from almost anywhere, even when there is poor weather.[16]

But camera operators will tell you that the box is not the "end all" to broadcast problems. If you are the last crew to arrive at a scene, when you try to shoot in a signal, you'll often have the worst signal or no signal. (When this happens the picture often freezes up or breaks up or becomes pixilated in such a manner that the signal is unacceptable for broadcast.) Even so, the Dejero box has become the answer to many problems broadcasters face when attempting to go live, quickly, in difficult situations.

In May 2012, a major planned event turned into breaking news: the NATO summit. If there was ever an event tailor-made for using the Dejero box, this was it. Television stations began planning months in advance for the event because groups of anarchists had shown up at previous NATO events and caused widespread looting, rioting, and other antisocial activities. Chicago would be center stage.[17]

While Dejero technology had been around for a few years, on a small scale—used at Olympic coverage and other planned events—the NATO summit would be the first field test of the live apparatus in sometimes hostile and unpredictable situations. There were thousands of protesters in downtown Chicago speaking out about economic concerns, among other matters.[18]

Camerapeople using the Dejero box at the demonstration found themselves working very hard to provide a live signal back to the newsroom. Since most camerapeople were one-man bands, their task of trying to pull a hand truck (a small L-shaped handcart with two wheels and two handles) while also wearing a heavy backpack containing a Dejero box *and* shooting a large, broadcast-style camera as they weaved and bumped down the crowded street was, at best, a torturous experience lasting most of the day.

In Chicago, this was the maiden voyage for live cell phone transmissions. The video sent back to the newsrooms across the city was choppy, unstable, and often broke up in the middle of a shot. Yet when a cameraperson was able to keep up with the action, he or she sent back astounding live pictures that had never been seen before from inside a protest march—showing the demonstrators as they moved through Chicago and allowing viewers to see the action and hear the protest songs and angry, vitriolic chants as police and demonstrators stood eye to eye during many hateful confrontations.

BROADCASTING GROWS—PUBLISHING SLOWS

As broadcast news continues to morph into an entity that some say is no longer a dinosaur, it is clear that those running television companies think something altogether different. Owning a television station has long been equated to having a legalized method of printing money. In major markets, newspapers may be dying because of shrinking readership and revenues, but television is alive and well. (Television stations now have their websites as a new source of revenue; advertisers spend large sums supporting Internet ads.)

Audience considerations are built into the news making process in a variety of ways. For example, Tribune Company Broadcasting, the parent company of WGN-TV, has been acquiring television stations over the last thirty years. By 2013, Tribune had twenty-three stations just before it announced that it would buy nearly twenty broadcast TV stations from Local TV Holdings for about $2.7 billion. The deal would make Tribune one of the biggest TV station owners in the country.[19] Eventually Tribune management says the publishing and television groups will split and form two separate entities.[20]

WHAT THE VIEWING PATTERNS MEAN

While the central concern of journalists is creating the news, implicit understandings of the audience are embedded in both the news values of evaluating different murder victims journalists cover and in the technology they use. In the case of spot news, the broadcast journalist and his organization's emphasis on live news reporting is based on implicit assumptions that audience members deem live reporting more important, timely, and credible than other forms of reporting. Normally, murder stories will be covered "live" to give the story more immediacy. Whether those assumptions are accurate or not, they do contribute to the way the stories are presented.

Images of the audience are not easily detected because the audience is not explicitly addressed very often—nor is the audience homogenous. Yet it is a mistake to therefore assume that the audience is not an important component of the news construction process. Understandings about the audience are built into news values in much the way implicit news values are built into the news process. For example, as illustrated, timeliness becomes a key consideration in the broadcast news formula, often taking precedence over depth of analysis. Many times all a reporter needs to do is report from the scene that a murder has taken place. And because the murder is being covered "live," it gives it a certain "importance." Implicit in that elevation of the "timeliness" news value is an understanding that the audience turns to TV or radio or a mobile device (Twitter) for the latest details, not for substantive interpretative reporting (unless viewers are watching PBS). There is little if any discussion among news workers during a breaking news story (let's say a shooting) about what caused the shooting and why. However, that understanding undergirds what they do. In follow-up versions of the story—even later in the newscast—reporters may try to supply more in-depth information about the event.

Chapter Eight
PERSPECTIVE AND TRUTH

Everything we hear is an opinion, not a fact. Everything we see is a perspective, not the truth.

—Marcus Aurelius

Your perspective is the way you see something. If you think that television corrupts children's minds, then from your perspective a television station is a wicked place. Economist Fabian Linden once said, "It is useful occasionally to look at the past to gain a perspective on the present."[1] When we examine the way murder cases have been handled in the past, we can't help but come away with the conclusion that the process is uneven at best and embarrassingly one-sided at its worst.

For news gatekeepers, perspective may present the biggest challenge they face on a daily basis, when assessing murder stories. No two people working in a news setting are likely to have identical perspectives on anything. And the only way to work toward a common perspective—aiming for the truth—is to continually remind ourselves that we are flawed creatures in need of constant reinforcement of our shared journalistic values and beliefs. Yet, even this attempt at arriving at the least common denominator of "points of view" is difficult and depends on many disparate factors.

Which is bigger: a tornado smashing through a small Midwestern town, leveling hundreds of homes, or the murders of nine church members by twenty-one-year-old white supremacist Dylann Storm Roof? Without a doubt, the Roof story catches the most national attention. But if you live in that shell-shocked, tornado-ravaged town, what Dylann Roof did is not your immediate concern. Your perspective on what is the big story of the day is much different from someone living in Charleston, South Carolina.

Yet, even though our news sensibilities are mostly jaded from overkill of so-called "breaking news," at some point our cynical and worn-out emotional responses cause us to say, "Enough is enough! This is where I draw the line." An event so unthinkable, that it shocks us to the core, often produces profound consequences.

Such a moment occurred during the week of June 17, 2015, when news broke that Roof confessed to killing nine people at a historic black church in Charleston, South Carolina, because he hoped it would start a "race war."[2]

But what gave this episode such a sad, sorry, and sensational twist was the fact that Roof was white—not black. Had the same awful crimes been committed by a black man looking for drug money, the story would not have captured the national and international stage the way it did. Our perspectives would have been different.

And before you say, "That just isn't so," consider this: in 2014, just a year before the Charleston shootings of nine people—in Chicago, over the Fourth of July weekend—fourteen people were murdered and eighty-two were shot.[3] Yet not many people outside Chicago even knew these horrible statistics existed. Most of the shooters were black, and most of the victims were black, so not much was done in the media to alert the public to these ghastly figures. That's like a marching band—eighty-two people—parading down the street. Let's not kid ourselves—if eighty-two white people had been shot over the same weekend, we'd still be reporting on the crimes and talking about it a year later. So there is a real double standard—a big difference in perspective—about the importance of lives. Black lives are not deemed to be as important as white lives; they are second-rate murders.

We judge the awfulness of an event by taking into consideration not just the nature of the crime but many other elements, as well. In the case of the murders at Emanuel African Methodist Episcopal (AME) Church in Charleston, Roof's idiotic aim was to provoke a race war. There were also other essential elements in the story: the profile of the victims—mostly elderly "God-fearing" female church members, as well as a well-loved, high-profile church minister who was also a state senator—and the cold-blooded nature of the execution-style murders. Additionally, the crime scene was in a historic, revered black church in Charleston—a city that has long stood as a beacon of racial intolerance, dating back to the days of slavery. All these elements contributed to the atrociousness of the crime—and the prolific coverage. In fact, not far from the church, in the old town square, is the location where slaves were sold at auction. Roof knew all these things and took them into consideration before he pulled the trigger on his first victim.[4]

As horrible as this case is, I bring it into this discussion because there is much to be learned from this dreadful, diabolical incident—a moment in time so abhorrent that it must be considered a sickening milestone in the history of crime and race relations in America.

There are way too many examples of a clear disparity in the way news organizations cover stories that involve people of color. Sometimes the numbers of victims and those injured are staggering, yet because the victims are minority and poor, they are mostly ignored.

Take the example of the blistering Chicago heat wave of 1995 when more than seven hundred people died over the span of four days[5]—more than twice as many deaths as the Great Chicago Fire of 1871, which almost leveled the entire city. Those seven hundred victims were mostly elderly, poor, and black—an ignominious combination almost certain to lead to social invisibility.

Since the Chicago media slept through this disaster, city officials knew they had dodged a public relations bullet. So afterward, plans were quickly put into place so the city would be prepared in case a similar heat wave returned. Now when the temperature reaches past ninety degrees, city workers check up on the elderly, and city buildings are converted into "cooling centers" with the air-conditioning turned on.[6]

During the crisis, former mayor Richard Daley hoped to use ComEd (the electricity supplier) and its system as a way to alert city officials of power outages in the hot summer months. "We've learned a lot, not only in Chicago but throughout the country and throughout the world, how dangerous heat is," Daley said.[7]

I remember working the streets that weekend in 1995 when the heat wave began taking its toll. My cameraman, Pat O'Keefe, and I had been working on another story and driving around Chicago in the minicam truck. When we turned up the volume on the police and fire scanner, all we heard were police and paramedics arriving at different hospitals with victims—dead on arrival. And while the following are not actual calls, this is the way it sounded:

"Ambulance 23 at Cook County Hospital with DOA."
"Squad 54 at County Hospital with a DOA."
"Ambulance 22 at County with a DOA."
"Squad 56 at Jackson Park Hospital with a DOA."

The scanner chatter was incessant. I looked at Pat, and we realized that something way out of the ordinary was going on. I called my station and talked to the assignment desk and the news producer that day. I told them, "I'm listening to the scanners, and something's crazy—people are dropping like flies. There are nonstop calls of ambulances arriving at hospitals around the city with DOAs."

We were told to continue working on the story we had begun and that they would look into it. Like every other television and radio station in town, we blew that story, because it wasn't until days later, when the morgue was filled to capacity and the medical examiner had brought in refrigerated eighteen-wheel trucks to stack the bodies, that the media began to notice the enormity of the event.

I also remember the sad ending to this tragic story. One day I was sent to cover the burial of the unclaimed bodies from the coroner's office. Many of the victims of the heat wave died alone in their sweltering apartments and were buried the same way—without family or friends to mourn their deaths. In all, forty-one, mostly elderly people, were buried in a 160-foot-long mass grave in Homewood Memorial Gardens. The mass burial brought an even sadder ending to a sorrowful, tragic event that changed how the city deals with heat emergencies.[8]

THE SURPRISE OF UNINTENDED CONSEQUENCES

So often when events are so outrageous and "over the top," they have an opposite effect from the one intended by the perpetrator. Dylann Roof had hoped his actions would start a race war. Instead, a jury in Charleston, South Carolina, found Roof guilty on all thirty-three counts of federal hate crimes he faced for murdering nine people and attempting to kill three others in the basement of the historically black church.

Contrary to what Roof had hoped, blacks and whites in Charleston joined hands in a show of solidarity that has never existed before. White citizens, who were just as horrified as black church members, came to the church by the thousands to demonstrate their support and to show that they were not hateful racists, just because they were white.[9] A common perspective emerged about the importance of racial harmony.

Television stations in Charleston covered the story nonstop. Local reporters also appeared on national newscasts to augment the coverage that the networks were doing. This was a huge story, and local stations went out of the way to make sure that African American citizens were given ample opportunity to respond with dignity and grace. During such a horrible event it was refreshing to see how news outlets covered all sides of the story—not just chastising Roof but giving a deeper understanding of the African American community that formed the congregation of the historic church, and that community's reaction.

There was also an unintended consequence of the racial attacks. News reports showed Roof on his website holding a Confederate battle flag—the same one flying on the grounds of the state capitol in Columbia. Once these photos became publicized, the once-revered—in some circles—symbol of Southern heritage and white supremacy became abhorrent for most Southerners, many of whom had, before, supported the display of the flag as a symbol of "historic pride." A wave of indignation swept the nation, and the Confederate flag began coming down in businesses and homes. The trend continues.[10]

But African Americans had been trying for decades to have the Confederate flag taken down from places of prominence, saying it stood for and represented a hurtful period in the history of this country. Yet Southern politicians wouldn't budge, knowing that their chances of reelection would be in danger if they supported removing the Confederate flag. But after this incident, many so-called hard-liners began agreeing that the flag should come down. Even long-term, well-known conservative politicians jumped ship and are calling for the flag to be brought down and placed in a museum.

The widespread change in sentiment among many Charleston residents only occurred because of the in-depth reporting of local newspapers and television stations. Their unprecedented total immersion into the soul of the black community in Charleston gave the rest of the city and the nation a clear taste of what it was like to be a minority living in the South in 2015.

This was a rare opportunity to observe deep-seated mores begin to change because of social forces, prompted by the uproar of once-quiet voices—quiet voices that only were heard because media outlets decided the story merited coverage. White and black citizens who once hung in the shadows were slapped out of their sluggish malaise by the unbelievable brutality of Dylann Roof. They now understood that symbols can have upsetting and unkind meanings that cut deep into those who are the subjects of the intended nastiness.

In Charleston, blacks and whites have labored under a false premise that racial accord was the norm, partially because television newsrooms only told stories that promulgated that misconception. But now well-meaning neighbors have been forced to confront the uncomfortable truth, which is that old, ugly prejudices lie just below a thin veneer composed of a false belief that congeniality is everywhere. That uncomfortable truth came to light once reporters were able to dig deeper into the social structure of the city. The stories that aired on local newscasts uncovered the real Charleston and allowed all residents to learn about each other like never before: a healthy, productive, and truthful understanding about each other that produced a sometimes uncomfortable but needed revelation about racial division.

Roof made us all confront our concealed bigotries. None of us is pure, and though we may profess to be without racial hatred, we need only give ourselves time before we let it slip that we may despise someone who is gay or of another religion . . . or older or speaks another language . . . or who has more money or who dresses differently . . . or who is obese or is deformed or has a different skin color than us.

Once we make this admission and accept that we all have frailties and flaws, and that we observe our perspectives through different lenses, we can begin to see events differently, approaching similar points of view. These are the difficult news stories to tell—they require work and digging for thoughtful sources. They can rarely be produced in the time it takes to drive across town.

When news outlets cover the rape and beating of a woman from a leafy neighborhood in the suburbs, we should also consider women in other less affluent parts of town who are being abused and question why our perspectives about these victims are different: why aren't we as eager to hear about their struggles? You can be sure that episodes of rape and brutality are ubiquitous.

Some will argue that the nature of news is to look for unusual events. An example often cited is that "we cover plane crashes, not the fact that thousands of planes land safely each day." That is true. But news outlets also do investigative reports where reporters go in search of evidence that some long-term wrong is occurring and needs to be corrected. Likewise reporters can be more careful in judging the merit of stories selected and not just go for the "quick and dirty." Ava Greenwell goes over this point with her journalism students, telling them about a time when she was a television reporter:

> The issue isn't whether you're going to cover [a story], or which one you're going to cover, but how are you going to cover it?
>
> So, for instance, there had been a woman found murdered right at Seventy-Ninth and Calumet in Park Manor. There was a grocery store at Seventy-Nine near Ruggles Elementary School. So I went to the assignment desk, and I said, "Are you going to cover this?" I was just curious. They said no, we're not going to do anything with this. And I thought to myself, "Wait a minute, here's a dead woman—this is my neighborhood." So this time I'm biased and you're not going to do anything with it? Nothing?[11]

Greenwell says that being a double minority—a woman and black—she is conscious that stations sometimes don't urge their reporters to seek diversity when telling a story. When only white witnesses are the sole witnesses, that skews the story by not rounding out the subjects you interview:

I know when I was a reporter, when I was covering a story about the flu, I used to look for, say, a Latina doctor or a black physician or someone who could add substance to the story who wasn't the traditional face that we see telling stories all the time. That adds balance to every story, and that's the point we try to make. It really has to do with race and gender and equity issues, and every class should have something to do with race and gender because if you are a reporter and you're covering Chicago, it has to.

And there has to be an acceptance that the Internet is also very important to the success of a news program. And since web producers can see exactly who is visiting their station's website and for how long, producers have a definitive tool for judging which stories are popular and which ones may not be, as we discussed in a previous chapter. Web producer Anna Roberts is one of several people who places material on the WGN-TV website each day. Roberts is always adjusting the content and has broad power over what is added or taken down from the site:

I want to think that we're selling a site—that's what my bosses worry about more than I do. I want to be helping the site be popular and good and reliable and that sort of thing. [It's] why we want to do this anyway—the boost you get for being part of that. So, yeah, even if we have 110 stories all about less flashy topics—government stuff, pension stuff, budget, all of the city council stories we know—unless there is something that sticks out like a parking meter thing, a lot of that is not very clickable for people. So we will post it, but it won't be highlighted as much as other stories that we know.

Localization and "on demand" programming are changing the way news stations are covering stories. But if news outlets are to survive in this changing marketplace, they need to remember one of the most important reasons for telling stories—the audience.

DO PEOPLE BUY THE DRILL OR THE HOLE?

When thinking about how news outlets can remain viable in this changing environment, the drill vs. hole epigram comes to mind. I'm talking about the famous quote often attributed to Harvard Business School professor Theodore Levitt: "People don't want to buy a quarter-inch drill. They want to buy a quarter-inch hole!" That simple witticism demonstrates how lost we can become in our search for truth.

Just as difficult as it is to accept that the church massacre in Charleston would not have been such a major story if a black man had been the shooter, there are also other realities that exist concerning the manner of covering news stories. The statement "they want a hole" focuses us on a more realistic way of aiming our energies in the proper direction.

In earlier chapters I talked about the shrinking newspaper industry and the continued loss of viewers on broadcast television. Not too long ago television was a growth industry. As computers, cell phones, laptops, and mobile devices continue to chip away at audiences, television is trying to reinvent itself.

In every case, the reason industrial growth stagnates is not because the market is saturated. It is because there has not been a new, creative way for reaching audiences. Thus, we can blame a failure of management. Producers and news managers can learn from the example of the railroads, as discussed in the following *Harvard Business Review* article:

> The railroads did not stop growing because the need for passenger and freight transportation declined. That grew. The railroads are in trouble today not because that need was filled by others (cars, trucks, airplanes, and even telephones) but because it was not filled by the railroads themselves. They let others take customers away from them because they assumed themselves to be in the railroad

business rather than in the transportation business. The reason they defined their industry incorrectly was that they were railroad oriented instead of transportation oriented; they were product oriented instead of customer oriented.[12]

In the case of newsrooms, the customers are the viewers, listeners, or readers, and their needs have to be addressed fairly and accurately. Providing viewers with a false sense of what is important—based on specious rationales—will eventually drive the audience away.

And while the paradigm for delivering news is changing at lightning speeds, for the immediate future, mobile devices seem to be the platform for those interested in news. A Pew Research study claims that a large number of smartphone users rely on their phones to receive breaking news near them or far away.[13] The study also found the following:

- 68 percent of smartphone owners use their phone at least occasionally to follow along with breaking news events, with 33 percent saying that they do this "frequently."
- 67 percent use their phone to share pictures, videos, or commentary about events happening in their community, with 35 percent doing so frequently.
- 56 percent use their phone at least occasionally to learn about community events or activities, with 18 percent doing this "frequently."[14]

With so many smartphone apps devoted to news and events of the day, news organizations have begun to insist that reporters do double duty. As soon as they file the story they were sent to cover, they immediately use their phones to grab a significant photo of the scene and then send a quick report to the station website. Sometimes this is done before the reporter begins working on the story for the later news show. Even television anchors are being asked to use Twitter or Facebook during commercial breaks to answer viewers' questions and reply to comment sections so the viewer will feel "more connected" to the anchors. It's like personalizing the newscast. My longtime coanchor, Jackie Bange, and I would always take a photo of ourselves and list some "clever" caption on the photo. Our viewers would respond right away, and each entry would receive thousands of views.

As noted earlier, WGN-TV has begun to place a high regard in how the station uses the Internet for both disseminating news and attracting viewers to the station. Web producer Elyse Russo knows management views her job as essential. "I think that's because our news director and assistant news director see the importance of having a story online and having it accurate, in first if it can," Russo says. "I think [that] having it first and accurate makes people want to come to us—not only for our written content but also for our video content. I do think they see it as important."[15]

Television stations face a unique challenge. Their market shares are shrinking while their viewers are growing. How is this possible? Let's take a hypothetical one thousand viewers who were watching a television station in 1960. During that year 100 percent of viewers were tuned into Channel 9 to see their news. Today, the number from that same group watching Channel 9 over the airwaves might be one hundred or fewer, even though there are still one thousand people seeing the WGN-TV product. They're just watching on their cell phones and laptops (over the Internet) and seeing their programs at a different time because they were recorded (by DVR). In the case of the big networks, some viewers are streaming the shows as on demand programming.

This spiderweb of ways to watch television has disrupted the way television was originally sent into homes. All this change has happened in a matter of a few years—not decades. So broadcast television, which used to be considered a way to almost print your own money, is, in some markets, struggling to make a huge profit. Viewers are still tuning into local stations like WGN-TV, but a large percentage are doing so over different mediums—some of which are free: cell phones, laptops, etc. The *Harvard Business Review* states,

> The belief that profits are assured by an expanding and more affluent population is dear to the heart of every industry. It takes the edge off the apprehensions everybody understandably feels about the future. If consumers are multiplying and also buying more of your product or service, you can face the future with considerably more comfort than if the market were shrinking. An expanding market keeps the manufacturer from having to think very hard or imaginatively. If thinking is an intellectual response to a problem, then the absence of a problem leads to the absence of thinking. If your product has an automatically expanding market, then you will not give much thought to how to expand it.[16]

Unfortunately, just the opposite is occurring in television and newspapers. These hard times have produced desperate measures to compete in a field where so much of your product is being viewed almost for free (or in a manner that is not producing revenue for the station).

Many of these frantic efforts to turn around a struggling industry have produced an emphasis on violent crime and dramatic events as a way to grab an audience. Murders, as we discussed earlier, are basically easy to cover because most of the time there is little to report since little is known. *Ex nihilo nihil fit* means "nothing comes from nothing." Instead, I argue that the news director's task is to understand the "job" (overseeing the delivery of accurate, compelling, and interesting news and information) the customer wants to see, and design products (newscasts) and brands that fill that need.

The job of delivering news is a complex one that forces participants to confront the subtleties and nuances of personal prejudices that many of us may not even know exist. News leaders must understand what the audience is tuning in for. For a local station to improve and increase its audience, station managers must gain a better understanding of the mission and aim of the newsroom and how the organization plans to move in that direction. Additionally, understanding how and why we cover the Charleston shootings with such fervor can open our eyes to the manner in which we report these kinds of tragedies and recognize some of the truths that come out of heartbreaking stories like these.

When delivering a eulogy for his friend, state senator Rev. Clementa Pinckney, President Barack Obama gave a passionate and, at times, touching speech. "None of us can or should expect a transformation in race relations overnight," Obama said. "Every time something like this happens, somebody says, 'We have to have a conversation about race.' . . . We talk a lot about race. There's no shortcut. We don't need more talk."[17]

And as has been brought out in this chapter, we must remember that there are shades and degrees of prejudices that steer our thoughts and actions. Obama put it this way: "Maybe we now realize the way a racial bias can infect us even when we don't realize it so that we're guarding against not just racial slurs, but we're also guarding against the subtle impulse to call Johnny back for a job interview but not Jamal."[18]

Undoubtedly, Roof will join the pantheon of diabolical, bloodthirsty killers who make up the gallery of history's most notorious criminals: Charles Manson, Jeffrey Dahmer, Al Capone, Brian Mitchell, David Berkowitz, Susan Smith, and O. J. Simpson.

Unintentionally, Roof has caused many journalists and other people to stop and examine their actions and deeds and thoughts in a way they have never done before. Its's just a shame that it took such a terrible and sorrowful act for these realizations to take place.

Chapter Nine

REALIGNING THE PROCESS FOR COVERING MURDERS

If we are to go forward today, we've got to go back and rediscover some mighty precious values that we've left behind. That's the only way that we can make our world a better world.

—Martin Luther King Jr., "Rediscovering Lost Values" sermon, February 24, 1954

As a teenager, beginning to sense the surging testosterone coursing through my body, I would try to push the moral boundaries my parents had set up, inquiring why I couldn't do all the things my buddies were doing—staying out late or going to all the parties they attended. To whom I then considered my old-fashioned and out-of-touch parents, I would repeatedly say that "times have changed." My mother would always respond that times may have changed but morals and scruples shouldn't. I never had a suitable rebuttal for that truism.

As we've seen in the preceding chapters, changing times have marginally improved the manner in which people of color are covered in the news. Even so, there is a wide gap in how black and white citizens are given news coverage and how each group is portrayed in that coverage.

Why is this important? We all depend on information flow to keep us informed on daily events: fighting in the Middle East, a teachers' strike that will close schools, or tornados heading toward a farm town in Iowa. Armed with knowledge that certain events are imminent, we can make smart decisions that may involve life and death.

Likewise, beliefs that the information is accurate and unbiased are essential if the audience is to trust and rely on that material. We have learned over the decades to have "blind faith" in the veracity of news reports because we understand dedicated journalists to be thoughtful, sincere, and fair. But today journalists face enormous pressures from a changing paradigm of information dissemination: more direct interpersonal communication between the journalist and audience (e.g., comments sections and e-mails). They also face labor force shortages; increased job responsibilities; younger, less experienced professionals assuming critically important senior roles (heretofore held by seasoned experts); rapidly changing technology that allows instantaneous, worldwide dissemination of information; and the biggest change of all—anyone and everyone can do it. That's good, bad, and scary!

Today, no one would argue with you if you said that journalism has changed, especially broadcast news workers. The manner of dispersing news and information is no way similar to how our parents or grandparents received their news, whether it was in print, radio, or television. First of all, the swiftness with which information is transmitted today is at the speed of light, not measured in terms of hours or days, as it was just a decade or two ago.

We marvel, now, when we look back at thoughtful journalists like Bill Kovach and Tom Rosenstiel, who in 1999 published a visionary book that warned about a "new mixed-media culture" that was composed of these elements:

- A never-ending news cycle making journalism less complete
- Sources gaining power over journalists
- No more gatekeepers

- Argument overwhelming reporting
- A "blockbuster" mentality taking over[1]

Some of those characteristics are true today; there are still gate-keepers, but there is almost a never-ending news cycle. (When Rosenstiel and Kovach went to press in 1999, Ted Turner had already begun his twenty-four-hour news operation, CNN, which debuted in 1980.) When I started at WGN-TV in 1973, we produced one hour of news five days a week: thirty minutes at 5:00 p.m. and thirty minutes at 10:00 p.m. Now the station produces thirteen hours each day, Monday through Friday, and eight hours on the weekends—more in one day than we produced, back then, in a week. So many other channels have gone to round-the-clock news operations that you can't keep count.

THE WAY NEWS IS COVERED HAS CHANGED WHAT'S NEWS

What Bill Kovach and Tom Rosenstiel didn't predict was how the content of broadcast news would morph from a broad menu of all kinds of news stories into a nearly singular dependence on "blood-and-guts" stories. "If it bleeds it leads," the laughable axiom of the 1970s and 1980s, is truer today than ever before. These easy-to-produce and shallow-in-content items fill the first two segments of most TV newscasts: murders, car crashes, and violent confrontations that result in life-threatening injuries or death.

Much of the content is shown live, from poor minority neighborhoods. And since little effort is made to tell the other side of the minority story, unsophisticated viewers are given a distorted, myopic view of whom these Chicagoans are. This leaves viewers thinking that what they're seeing is representative of all African American and

Latino citizens. Dr. Carl Bell, psychiatrist, says the feeling to look down on the "others" is inherent in us all and is built into our mental wiring.

The additional concern, Bell says, deals with journalists themselves, that they "are looking not to get their stories killed and they kind of have this understanding that in order not to get the story killed it's got to be interesting . . . to make the viewer, the reader remain and stay on the story. And so there is a tendency to want to focus on the unusual as opposed to the ordinary or the average."[2]

Ava Thompson Greenwell says she spends quite a bit of time with her Medill journalism students going over the importance of looking more deeply at race and socioeconomic realities that are sometimes brushed over lightly:

> Most of the kids in this class are white students, and so I'm not preaching to the choir necessarily. But, these are also the students we're going to be moving into these [leadership] positions, and we can't just assume that because a student is also a person of color that they are understanding of that experience. Because I also had a student—an African American student—who had grown up in a predominantly white neighborhood, and I don't think he was coming to grips with his racial identity until he came here. And so it was still important for him to understand these things because he really hadn't been exposed to them before.[3]

Greenwell was a television reporter before she began teaching at Medill and knows how newsroom demands for quick returns on stories often force reporters to be shallow. She teaches her students that the better method is to look for a way to expand the story and give meaning to an issue, helping the audience learn more about a subject. "[W]e don't really get into covering the stories the way they should," Greenwell notes. "But nobody has taken the time to really say, 'Okay, if the police are saying the shootings are contained to certain zip codes and certain blocks, then let's make sure that in our reporting we clarify that, so we don't think the entire South Side is this bastion of shooting.'"[4]

Greg Caputo, who has been a television news journalist for over forty years and a news director for most of that time, knows just how important it is to have a deeply integrated staff, from producers and writers to reporters and camera crews:

> Forget about [whether] this is a good thing or bad thing morally. In order for you to do the job that you are getting paid to do, you have to have some sort of diversity in the staff making those decisions. That needs to get better across the board—that has never been good, even in my early days of television. Certainly in our early days of television that was not the case—when I started [in] my early days in WBBM, they had no female reporters.[5]

A BROADER, MORE DIVERSE STAFF IMPROVES THE NEWS CONTENT

Having a varied, diverse staff that reflects its audience helps ensure a more authentic journalistic product. Heretofore, African Americans and Latinos were often the stars of the perfunctory "perp walk"—suspects, handcuffed together, being marched from city jail to the courthouse. Today news executives have seen increased viewership in certain minority demographics, such as Latinos, and hope to make them permanent loyal viewers. According to the Pew Research Journalism Project, Hispanic Americans are causing a major shift in the viewing demographics. As one of the fastest-growing groups in the United States, the population has grown from 50 percent in 2000 to 2012, growing to fifty-three million people. And while there are continuing cries for checks to stop the inflow of the immigrant population, Pew cites that most of that growth has come from births in the United States rather than new immigrants—legal and illegal.[6]

Recently, Chicago media observer Robert Feder published a column that listed the results of the June 2017 ratings battle. For the first time, the local Spanish language station—Univision—WGBO Channel 66 Chicago nearly edged out perennial leader, ABC's WLS Channel 7, losing by a fraction of a point. This is significant because it shows the gains in viewership, in recent years, that indicate a huge shift in viewer trends. For decades, in Chicago, Spanish language station numbers were almost always in the basement. But this ratings month, WGBO nearly won the competition.[7]

So, if news executives read and learn about these new demographic shifts, blacks and Hispanics in Chicago may begin to see people who look like them on television in situations other than "perp walks." When Ava Greenwell talks to her colleagues at Medill, she senses that most of them have rarely ventured into some of the tough minority neighborhoods that ring downtown Chicago. Yet they're expecting students to come away with an erudite understanding. That realization prompted Greenwell to take drastic action to give her journalism students a look inside the fishbowl to see that not every person in a scary neighborhood is dangerous:

> If I didn't know better, I would think that the entire South Side is nothing but places where shootings take place. And many of the students I have now for the spring quarter . . . I actually rented a van and took them on a trip riding around the South Side so that they could see and have a better idea about the area they were hearing about. So that they could see the place where Hadiya Pendleton was shot, I took them to Hyde Park.[8]

In previous chapters we've heard from assignment editors and producers who have talked about their reasons for shunning "cheap" murders—ones developing out of malice between gang members—because they happen too often and no longer are news. That rationale is controversial.

Pulitzer Prize–winning author Jack Fuller is the former editor and publisher of the *Chicago Tribune*. In his latest book, *What Is Happening to News: The Information Explosion and the Crisis in Journalism*, Fuller looks at the competition between stories on the Internet—on Twitter, Facebook, etc.—and understands that different types of stories will appeal to different readers and viewers. He relates how Joseph Pulitzer would argue that he used sensationalism on his front page to lure people into the heart of the paper—especially the editorial page—where they would be educated. But Fuller questions that approach, saying, "I'm not sure this ever worked. But, today, it is not a strategy that makes any sense. Every story needs to fight for attention on its own, and the more important the story, the harder it should fight."[9]

If Fuller is correct, then journalism gatekeepers need not fret over determining which murder story is more important than the other: just cover them all. Some newspapers and websites are actually doing this. At the *Chicago Sun-Times*, reporter Michael Lansu follows each murder:

> Because we're doing it online, it really does give us a platform to do it. And when it gets busy, I'm also using the Internet to reach out to people. Sometimes you think you have a home address for a victim and you get there and it's a vacant lot—what do you do then? Well, you ask around the block, a little bit, and people say, "No, I don't know—I don't know him." Or, "He used to live here a couple of years ago." If you're on a deadline, that could be the end of your story that day. But I have the advantage of not having a daily deadline to do it on—which helps. And I can use social media to look on Facebook, to look on Twitter, to see if anyone is talking about him, and use the Internet to reach out to people that way.[10]

But if television stations changed formats and went to a style of covering murder after murder after murder, viewers would flee that channel in a heartbeat. Even at cable stations where standards are not as stringent and are more laid back, no program director would attempt to produce a show with a diet of nothing but murders. Who would be your audience . . . serial killers? So what's the answer? How do we begin to realign our thinking so that our news coverage is more complete and less snobbish?

First we have to realize a transformation is already underway—and has been for a few years—in how news is gathered, produced, and dispersed. The "good ol' days" are over.

Citizen journalists, armed with cell phone cameras, are radically changing the landscape. These individuals are capturing events as they happen and are adding a deeper dimension to organizations' newsgathering capabilities. Since a television station cannot post photographers everywhere to record potential news stories, and no one can predict with certainty where the next exploding event will occur, ad hoc civilians are using their personal cameras to record some of the biggest news stories that—without the existence of their video—wouldn't have been covered. Two classic cases are the LA police beating of motorist Rodney King and the choke hold death of Eric Garner, who died in a scuffle with New York police officers.

Both of these deaths became national stories that provoked demonstrations, riots, and public discussion for months. In the case of Garner, cell phone video captured the confrontation from beginning to end—even showing Garner as he begged for relief, on the ground, saying, "I can't breathe, I can't breathe."[11]

But in this case, the fact that there was video of the incident didn't work to defuse the controversy—just the opposite happened. Most civilians who viewed the confrontation saw a large African American man standing with his arms up in a gesture of submission and compliance, just before he was grabbed around the neck from behind and taken down. On the ground, the battle for control continued until Garner died. And while an autopsy by the New York City medical examiner found that Mr. Garner's death was a homicide, the coroner found the officer's arm around Garner's neck did not damage his windpipe or neck bones.[12]

But police officers (and the grand jury) saw the confrontation differently from many civilians. Law enforcement personnel saw the man as a possible suspect being asked to "assume the position," either up against the wall or with his hands behind his back to be handcuffed. Police officers saw the man's refusal to comply as an act of taking the confrontation up a notch, to the next level, leading to a skirmish to get the subject to comply with a direct order.[13]

Both these cases wouldn't have become top-story, headline news if there hadn't been video of each incident. In all likelihood both cases would have been ignored as "routine" police killings that happen all the time. If the cases *had* somehow come to the attention of assignment editors, they would probably have relied on the version of events given by the police "public affairs office" that the death of Garner was justified as being in the line of duty. Rodney King's extensive beating never would have made the news had it not been for the video.

Realizing that these two cases are prime examples of how potentially important news stories can be overlooked, editors should be encouraged to begin paying more attention to the obscure cases that have a modicum of credibility. History has shown us that there are potential injustices more often than we think.

My concern is that if murders continue to decrease nationwide, editors may begin concentrating on other types of stories, knowing that the trend is on a downward slope.

CHOOSING STORY SUBJECTS IS EQUALLY IMPORTANT

This notion that we have a responsibility to let television news stories—that we build and sculpt through the process of selecting subjects to be interviewed—reflect the audience of the locale is seldom talked about in newsroom meetings. News officials must think that reporters and editors already know that keeping our reports "well rounded" is an underlying objective. But, too often, reporters turn in stories about black people with all-white interviewees. We wouldn't dare interview all men if we were discussing stories about ovarian cancer or pregnancy unless they were male physicians, and even then, that may be an affront. A certain journalistic sensitivity is often overlooked when it comes to minorities. And this lack of thoughtfulness causes some murder stories to stay out of the public's consciousness. Ava Greenwell says there's been a gradual realization that reporters have often committed this type of faux pas and that they haven't been called on it:

> When I was a student here at Medill there was this idea of objectivity. Yes, let's strive for that, but I think now that's shifted somewhat and students are being taught that objectivity is the goal. But the reality is, all of us bring certain baggage to the table—who we are, where we grew up, how we were raised; we can't ignore that. In fact it's important to recognize that for us, and then perhaps we can at least recognize am I being biased, here, in terms of the people I select. So, for example, I might tell students if you're going out to do a sports story, I don't want to see all males in a sports story, because there are women who are interested in sports as well.[14]

Many times assignment editors are caught up in the rush and pressures of the job. They are without a doubt the busiest employees in the newsroom and often carry on their shoulders the weight of the success or failure of the news coverage for that day. Assignment editor Chris Neale says,

Oh sure, we're feeding the beast here. It's not just WGN/CLTV, [but] it's the websites; it's the *Chicago Tribune* . . . [and] you take all of these news feeds in, and again, it makes it tougher in terms of perspective when, again, you got all the stories. What's the priority here? When you [meaning me—Robert Jordan] first started with WGN, you'd have all day to work on a story . . . a homicide story. But right now we can assign you to a murder story and you'd be expected to be on the air in an hour, right? . . . And it doesn't really lend to getting into the background, and what happened. And that's why I think we tend to write it off as, it's the same story or we ignored it totally.[15]

But in order to think "modern day" we must realize that sooner or later viewers are going to be turned off by the episodic nature of news coverage: a hot murder story today and then days of invisible victims who show up in the newscast, simply as the day's statistics. We've seen the scenario so many times where a person of some type of importance gets shot and killed (a baby, student, police officer, suburban homemaker, etc.) and the victim remains in the headlines for days or until the pressure on the case causes, inexplicably, a suspect to be arrested. A case in point is a story that dominated Chicago headlines, about Betty Howard, a beloved retired schoolteacher, who was killed by a stray bullet when a reported gang member was firing at a rival. She was fifty-eight years old.[16]

Betty Howard is a shining example of the type of murder victim whose death galvanizes a community. There was an outpouring of sympathy, indignation, and anger that someone who should have lived to a ripe old age was killed by a bonehead coward. The shooter stepped from the shadows, firing indiscriminately, striking her and killing her on the spot.

The death of Howard occurred while I was writing this chapter. As soon as I heard about the details of her tragic killing, I knew instantly that her case would soar to the top of the media agenda.

I also knew that it would be solved right away. Everyone wanted this shooter found and prosecuted. Consequently, police applied enormous pressure to local toughs. And sure enough, within a two-week period, police had arrested and charged a suspect.[17]

Residents of these high-crime neighborhoods know that police quickly solve the big cases. And police will tell you that many times the victims or their neighbors already know who the culprits are but refuse to step up and "rat" on the bad guy. Reporter Michael Lansu told me about a time when he knocked on the door to talk to family members of a man who had been shot and killed while the man was out shoveling snow. What he heard shocked him:

> She said she knew who shot and killed her son. Now, she didn't see it—not from where the house was and where he was shoveling. But, it was a little community over there . . . kind of gated in, almost . . . it's a weird site. And, she said, "I know who shot my son." She just . . . told me the name, and she told me what gang he was in, and she kind of pointed—he lives over there. And I asked, "Did you tell police?" And she said, "No." Now, eventually she must've told police because the guy was captured a few days later. So, whether or not police talked to her right away or she went out of her way to contact police or police came back [no one knows for sure] . . . but she knew. And as hard as it is—everybody thinks how difficult it must be for families after somebody has been killed. Think about it: not only did your son just die, but you know who did it and he lives right around the corner, and you're probably going to see him multiple times before he's arrested.[18]

THE TIDE MAY BE TURNING

There is a little-known secret happening, quietly. Residents are beginning to alert police to the suspects. In some cases, they might not supply a name, but they will give enough information that police can put two and two together and come up with a suspect. And, as I said earlier, when the pressure is on, even gangs will give up the shooter; there's just too much police presence in the neighborhood. Former deputy superintendent Al Wysinger hopes to build trust with the communities:

> Actually, a perfect example of that is going back to having the same cops on the same beats every day. Actually getting the officers out of their vehicles and putting them back on foot patrols. We just had a press conference today about the addition of officers that we're going to put on bikes. We're going to have more bikes riding in the neighborhoods . . . giving them the opportunity to interact and get to know the people . . . to begin to start repairing some of those bridges and rebuilding that trust. The community seems to love it.
>
> So far we've had positive feedback where you can have an officer, a young officer, just walk up and ask you, "How are you doing today? How are things in the neighborhood? Anything you'd like to let us know about? How are your grandkids, [and] how are they doing?" And I got a chance to experience that firsthand last summer when we rode down with these foot officers in the Eleventh District, and I even actually walked their beat with them. It was a Friday when a lot of the kids were going to the proms. [We] let the community see us and engaged with them, and it was something that you really couldn't put into words . . . ten or fifteen minutes standing there and talking and taking pictures and congratulating them. By the time we were done with that, the family actually let us know that they had another son that was graduating the following Friday and asked us to come back just to be a part of that. So, just little things like that go a long way in the community, and they begin to trust us and build relationships.[19]

When it comes to paying tribute to the recently departed, Lansu can tell you about times when he has been warmly received and other times when he received the very cold shoulder. "I think certain gang members feel the same way about talking to the media, not all of them," Lansu says. "But, sometimes you'll get gang members who will talk to you and say wonderful things about somebody who died. And sometimes they want no part of it. And I don't know if that's a drug money thing, or a cultural thing within that gang, or neighborhood thing."[20]

Lansu, with a news staff of one, covers the city of Chicago 365 days a year. Most television stations have fifty times more people in the newsroom (although most aren't digging *only* into murders), yet a conscious decision is made to skip some murder stories and go after others.

Many times, when journalistic gatekeepers consider ethics, direct conflicts arise between the rights of one person or group and those of others. The decision they make inevitably must favor some to the exclusion of others. Often our most agonizing dilemmas revolve around our primary obligation to a person or social group. In their book, *Media Ethics: Cases and Moral Reasoning*, Clifford Christians, Mark Fackler, Kim Rotzoll, and Kathy McKee list five moral duties that journalists can take into consideration when making decisions about what to cover:

1. **Duty to Ourselves:** Maintaining our integrity and following our conscience may be the best alternative in many situations. However, "Careerism" is a serious professional problem and often tempts us to act out of our own self-interest while we claim to be following our conscience.
2. **Duty to Clients/Subscribers/Supporters:** If they pay the bills and if we sign contracts to work for them, do we not carry a special obligation to them? Even in the more amorphous matter of a viewing audience that pays no service fee for a broadcast signal, our duty to them must be addressed when we are deciding which course of action is the most appropriate.
3. **Duty to our Organization or Firm:** Often company policy is

followed much too blindly, yet loyalty to an employer can be a moral good. Whistle blowing, that is, exposing procedures or persons who are harming the company's reputation, is also morally relevant here. Reporters might even defy court orders and refuse to relinquish records in whistle-blowing cases, under the thesis that ultimately the sources on which media companies depend will dry up. Thus, duty to one's firm might conceivably take priority over duty to an individual or to a court.

4. **Duty to Professional Colleagues:** A practitioner's strongest obligation is often to colleagues doing similar work. Understandably, reporters tend to prize, most of all, their commitments to fellow reporters and their mutual standards of good reporting. Some even maintain an adversarial posture against editors and publishers, just short of violating the standards of accepted etiquette.

5. **Duty to Society:** This is an increasingly important dimension of applied ethics and has been highlighted for the media under the term *social responsibility*. Questions of privacy and confidentiality, for example, nearly always encounter claims about society's welfare over that of a particular person. The "public's right to know" has become a journalistic slogan.[21]

MURDER STORIES JUDGED FROM ETHICAL CONSIDERATIONS

Making moral decisions is often the last consideration gatekeepers have to make. Since many newspaper and broadcast operations are run by owners who constantly have the bottom line in view, journalistic decisions are sometimes tempered by business concerns.

Newsroom staff is often trimmed to the bone, making coverage of events in a city like Chicago difficult to achieve. Assignment editor Natalie Costa agrees:

Over the years . . . you see a drop-off in [labor force and crews]. It gets less and less, and that's a huge factor. . . . [I]t's almost like a logic game to move people around and get them from place to place. . . .

Sometimes you get a weekend where you log on to your computer and you see the *Tribune* headline: "30 People Shot in the Last Two Days." Look, I would go to all of those if I could. But that's a big story here; you've got thirty crime scenes to look at, and you just can't do it. It takes a lot of gambling, and it takes a lot of moving people around, hoping for the best, and . . . you don't always get what you need for a story.[22]

Michael Lansu, the reporter who covers each murder in Chicago, agrees that a shortage in staff is a problem, even though he still accomplishes his job of posting something about every murder victim:

In the old days there were more reporters and editors. If we had one hundred general assignment reporters sitting around looking for something to do, they'd be out covering every murder. If TV didn't have news deadlines to meet, they'd be out covering every murder. If it were a two-hour newscast you could cover a lot more. But the reality is with a thirty-five-page newspaper, these days, or fifty-page newspaper, these days, there's limited space in the paper; there's a limited number of reporters to cover it. And it's the same thing on TV: a limited number of cameramen and reporters. And a lot of these murders happen in the middle of the night. If there's not a reporter immediately available, in the middle of the night, it gets overlooked.[23]

But Lansu says many of the decisions made by assignment editors are practical and are made after the editors have "rolled the dice" and decided to go after one story over another. He adds, "You feel like there's a little bit of this attitude among assignment editors: well, there's a good chance we're not going to get anything . . . and with limited [reporters and crews] you know if you send somebody to a

Rahm Emanuel press conference what you are going to get—you're going to get video and quotes." Though, Lansu says that "if you send someone down to knock on the door of a dead guy . . . you really don't know what you're getting—it could be a great story, or you could come back with nothing. And you just wasted a resource for the day."[24]

This quandary causes gatekeepers to make decisions that sometimes cut out whole communities from the public eye. And that omission is worse if the meager coverage that is given shows segments of that overlooked group in primarily one way: as violent offenders. This leaves audiences poorly informed because so much valuable information is left out. So the disservice ends up affecting the entire audience—making citizens vulnerable to creating poor decisions about contemporary trends and about their needs because they are so misinformed.

Ava Thompson Greenwell says part of the problem stems from the journalists who are telling the stories today. By and large, they don't reflect minority viewers and may have a skewed perspective on life in the neighborhoods they're covering:

> So let's look at people who work in newsrooms today. There is an elitist attitude more than they want to say, or not—just because of where they grew up and came from, and where they live today. So, that's one of the reasons we don't see the stations doing that much about public transportation, right? Because most of the people don't take public transportation or if they do, it's because it's very convenient and they'll want to save the cost. So, if I live in the suburbs, chances are I'm not taking public transportation to the station because, number one, I don't know what my schedule is going to be if I'm working in news and so, therefore, if all my interaction is with other people who are coming from the suburbs—which tend to be at least middle class, probably predominantly white—then my orientation is not going to be the same as somebody who's spending time with relatives on the West Side—who knows if these shootings happened on a regular basis.

But the fixes to the journalistic dilemmas of deciding to cover some stories and overlook others can be moderated. Police superintendent Al Wysinger says a good way to change the thinking of assignment editors and producers is to do what the Chicago police do from time to time—Citizens Academy:

> [W]e actually bring some citizens in—some people from the community and officials and actually run them through some of the training . . . that we have to go through to become a Chicago police officer. And the interesting part of the course—the thing I get the most feedback from—is when we put them in the simulated shooting exercises and the targets pop up and things flash in front of the men. You have that split second to make that decision—how many of them fire at the wrong person? . . . [O]nce they're put in the shoes of the police officer, it's like, wow, we understand what it's like to make that mistake or how important and how difficult it is to have a split second to make a life-or-death decision, [and] actually be wrong. And they feel some of the pressure that the men and women who work the streets every day feel, and it's totally different from being in a contained environment and knowing that whatever happens . . . you're not going to get killed or be seriously injured. And it just gives them a whole different perspective and changes so many of their mindsets. So, maybe you can get some of these editors out to do some ride-alongs and visit some of these communities and see what it's like and get firsthand experience on what the community actually feels. I mean, do some impromptu interviews on crime . . . talk to the victims of the families and feel what some of the families are going through.[25]

Judging from my experience, Wysinger is absolutely 100 percent correct. Having producers go into the communities on a regular basis would, no doubt, change attitudes of those journalists who often make complicated decisions while sitting inside the newsroom. *But that's not likely to happen.* Many will tell you that they already know what it's like to cover crime stories because, "I did it several times while I was in school." Well, I find that statement to be specious because—working in operating rooms in and out of the army—I have witnessed the delivery of hundreds of babies, too.[26] But I don't profess to know what it feels like to give birth. "Inside" journalists need to go "to the streets" often if they expect to receive a well-rounded perspective on what it is like covering breaking news in a big, diverse, complicated city like Chicago. News director Jennifer Lyons says she struggles every day with how decisions are made to cover some murders and not others. "I've had so many conversations with reporters in the newsroom," Lyons says. "Days when we will put those stories in front of us and sit and take a look at it and say, 'Now that's somebody's child—that IS a story.' And you are conflicted as a human being when you look at those stories."[27]

Lyons is the mother of six children. She is also a deeply compassionate and thoughtful woman whom I have known for over twenty years. (At one time she was my producer of the weekend news.) So, as a news director, she constantly struggles with the issue of ignoring the cases of some victims while going after others:

> I watched a documentary on Father Pfleger about the violence, and what struck me was this woman was grieving, and she was talking about how she lost her child to violence, and she was just one of the many moms out there who've lost a child. And I don't know if it's my mother's perspective or what. But in the middle of the piece, she said that she went to an event at St. Sabina's and she wore a T-shirt with her lost child's picture on it. And she said she walked into a club [of mothers who had lost children to shootings] that she had no idea was out there. I'll never forget all of those moms.[28]

As I conclude this chapter and book, I would like to take the liberty to include the *Elements of Journalism*, as outlined by Bill Kovach and Tom Rosenstiel, and fold some of those tenets into a discourse by Confucius.

In this time of lightning-fast dissemination of data and information, those wishing to avoid the pitfalls of snap decisions and rationalizations that are made out of habit need to pause and reflect on an ancient manner of thinking. One mode of reasoning may hold the answer to how journalists can easily challenge sloppy thinking; it dates back to Confucius.

The Way (Tao) of great learning consists of three areas: making illustrious virtue manifest, renewing the people, and abiding in the highest good.[29]

Reporters, simply, have to begin by understanding the goal of the endeavor they are about to undertake. Otherwise, the journalist will be lost and not see his or her moral compass: left to stumble about aimlessly without a path.

Over the course of this book we have looked at several examples of how journalists—assignment editors and producers—in television newsrooms make decisions on which murders to cover. These subjective conclusions are mostly based on gut feelings that come from elements of news: immediacy, proximity, prominence, oddity, conflict, suspense, emotion, and consequence. And as the old paradigm continues to change shape, journalists must take into mind several considerations. If I could paraphrase what Confucius might say:

> The earliest writers and reporters who wished to make illustrious virtue manifest throughout the world all understood that journalism's first obligation is to the truth. Wishing to fortify that commitment to truth, journalism's first loyalty is to citizens. Wishing to be the watchdog of the citizens, they first regulated their families; those who wished to regulate their families would first cultivate their own persons; those who wished to cultivate their persons would first rectify their minds; those who wished to rectify their minds would first make their intentions sincere; those who wished to make their intentions sincere would first extend their knowledge; the extension of knowledge consists in the investigation of things.

When things are investigated, knowledge is extended. When knowledge is extended, the intention becomes sincere; when the intention becomes sincere, the mind is rectified; when the mind is rectified, one's own person is cultivated; when one's person is cultivated, the family will be regulated; when the family is regulated, the truth will be ordered; when the truth is well ordered, the world will be tranquil.[30]

Journalists, who search for the highest truth in heaven down to the reasoning of the common man, must all regard cultivation of their person as the first order of business. Confucius says, "There has never been a case when the root is in disorder and the end is nonetheless well ordered; there never has been a case in which that which is carefully nurtured wastes away, or that which is negligently tended, flourishes."[31] Confucius knew that ideas and perspectives need to be carefully scrutinized before significant decisions are made.

Such is the case with the reporting of news.

NOTES

PREFACE

1. Reynolds was convicted in 1995 on charges of criminal sexual abuse, child pornography, and obstruction of justice for having sex with a sixteen-year-old former campaign intern. Jason Meisner, *Chicago Tribune*, April 20, 2016, http://www.chicagotribune.com/news/local/breaking/ct-mel-reynolds-in-custody-20160420-story.html (accessed July 19, 2017).

2. "Reynolds, Mel," History, Art & Archives United States House of Representatives, http://history.house.gov/People/Detail/20307?ret=True (accessed July 28, 2017).

3. Mel Reynolds, in phone conversation with the author, March 2016.

INTRODUCTION

1. Rick Hampson, "Donald Trump's Attacks on the News Media: A Not-So-Short History," *USA Today*, March 10, 2016, https://www.usatoday.com/story/news/politics/onpolitics/2016/03/10/donald-trump-versus-the-media/81602878/ (accessed May 30, 2017).

CHAPTER ONE: SECOND-RATE MURDERS . . . REALLY?

1. Sandy Pudar, in interview with the author, August 5, 2013. At the time of this interview she was executive producer of the WGN-TV morning news. She is now assistant news director.

2. Jennifer Lyons, in interview with the author, July 16, 2013.

3. Jeremy Gorner, "Chicago Violence, Homicides, and Shootings up in 2015," *Chicago Tribune,* January 2, 2015, http:// www.chicagotribune.com/news/local/breaking/ct-chicago-police -violence-2015-met1-20160101-story.html (accessed May 26, 2017).

4. Steve Schmadeke, "Suspect in Hadiya's Killing Claims Gang Leader Forced Him to Shoot," *Chicago Tribune,* http://www .chicagotribune.com/news/local/breaking/ct-hadiya-pendleton -killing-court-met-20160322-story.html (accessed July 19, 2017).

5. Erica-Lynn Huberty, "The Truth about Jennifer Levin, Robert Chambers and 'The Preppy Murder,'" *amNewYork,* August 21, 2016, http://www.amny.com/opinion/the-truth-about-jennifer -levin-robert-chambers-and-the-preppy-murder-1.12200807 (accessed July 19, 2017).

6. C. J. Hughes, "Man Who Killed and Dismembered a Lost Boy, 8, Gets 40 Years to Life," *New York Times,* August 29, 2012, http://www.nytimes.com/2012/08/30/nyregion/levi-aron-is -sentenced-to-40-years-in-killing-of-leiby-kletzky-8.html (accessed July 19, 2017).

7. "Crime Rate in Los Angeles, California (CA): Murders, Rapes, Robberies, Assaults, Burglaries, Thefts, Auto Thefts, Arson, Law Enforcement Employees, Police Officers, Crime Map," City-Data.com, 2017, http://www.city-data.com/crime/crime-Los -Angeles-California.html#ixzz4iDeWldMh (accessed May 26, 2017).

8. Cook County Medical Examiner's Office (coroner) releases information to media outlets when requested. I made a phone call to the ME's office requesting information on the number of murder cases that day.

9. Information supplied by the Chicago Medical Examiner's Office via phone call.

10. Sister of Gino Angotti, in phone conversation with the author, February 13, 2013.

11. Rummana Hussain, "Alleged Hadiya Pendleton Killers Plead Not Guilty," *Homicide Watch Chicago*, March 28, 2013, http://homicides.suntimes.com/2013/04/05/alleged-hadiya-pendleton-killers-plead-not-guilty/ (accessed July 19, 2017).

12. Jeff Granich, in phone conversation with the author, March 28, 2013.

13. Superintendent Garry McCarthy press conference, April 21, 2014. McCarthy spoke after a graduation ceremony for new police officers at Navy Pier in Chicago.

14. "Heat Don Hoodies after Teen's Death," ESPN.com, March 24, 2012, http://www.espn.com/nba/truehoop/miamiheat/story/_/id/7728618/miami-heat-don-hoodies-response-death-teen-trayvon-martin (accessed July 19, 2017).

15. Mary Helt Gavin, "Skittles Tree at Church and Dodge," *Evanston Round Table,* July 31, 2013, http://evanstonroundtable.com/main.asp?FromHome=1&TypeID=1&ArticleID=7586&SectionID=4&SubSectionID=4 (accessed July 18, 2017).

16. LHT Consulting Group, http://www.lhtgroup-us.com/ (accessed July 19, 2017).

17. According to AC Nielsen Company, 95.2 percent of homes own a TV and most have some kind of device hooked up to their television. "Nielsen Estimates 116.4 Million TV Homes in the US for the 2015–16 TV Season," Nielsen, August 26, 2015, http://www.nielsen.com/us/en/insights/news/2015/nielsen-estimates-116-4-million-tv-homes-in-the-us-for-the-2015-16-tv-season.html (accessed September 28, 2015).

18. Andrew V. Papachristos, "Forty-Eight Years of Crime in Chicago: A Descriptive Analysis of Serious Crime Trends from 1965 to 2013" (working paper, Institution for Social and Policy Studies, Yale University, New Haven, 2013).

19. Amanda Wills and Sergio Hernandez, "500 Homicides. 9 Months. 1 American City," CNN.com, January 1, 2017, http://www

.cnn.com/2016/09/06/us/chicago-homicides-visual-guide/index
.html (accessed July 18, 2017).

20. Pat Curry, in interview with the author, August 15, 2013.

21. Whet Moser, "Chicago Isn't Just Segregated, It Basically Invented Modern Segregation," *Chicago Politics & City Life*, March 31, 2017, http://www.chicagomag.com/city-life/March-2017/Why -Is-Chicago-So-Segregated/ (accessed July 19, 2017).

22. Benjamin Snyder, "This Is How Much a Super Bowl 50 Ad Costs," *Fortune Sports*, January 26, 2016, http://fortune.com/ 2016/01/26/super-bowl-50-ad-cost/ (accessed February 5, 2016).

23. Elyse Russo, in interview with the author, September 20, 2013.

24. "Television Measurement," Nielsen, http://www.nielsen .com/ie/en/solutions/measurement/television.html (accessed January 2015).

25. Greg Caputo, in interview with the author, August 5, 2013.

26. Lyons, interview with the author.

27. Caputo, interview with the author.

28. William Kovach and Tom Rosenstiel, *The Elements of Journalism* (New York: Random House, July 24, 2001).

29. Stephan Benzkofer, "1974 Was a Deadly Year in Chicago: A Record 970 People Were Slain in the City," *Chicago Tribune*, July 8, 2012, http://articles.chicagotribune.com/2012-07-08/site/ct-per -flash-1974-murders-0708-20120708_1_first-homicides-deadly-year -chicago-police (accessed May 27, 2017).

30. Phil Kadner, "$30 Debt May Have Spurred Saw Attack," *Chicago Sun-Times*, August 24, 2013.

31. Jason Meisner and Jeremy Gorner, "Teen Pleads Guilty in Death of Woman Pushed down CTA Stairs," *Chicago Tribune*, April 12, 2013, http://articles.chicagotribune.com/2013-04-12/news/ chi-teen-pleads-guilty-in-death-of-woman-who-fell-down-cta-stairs -20130412_1_kimberly-katona-sally-katona-king-prince-watson (accessed July 25, 2017).

32. Assignment editors at WGN-TV and CLTV, in conversations with the author, 2013–2014.

33. Ibid.

34. Lyons, interview with the author.

35. Al Wysinger, in interview with the author, April 18, 2014.

36. A euphemistic way of saying some cases don't get the same treatment as others.

37. Kalyn Belsha, "What It's like to Work for Rahm Emanuel," *Timeout Chicago*, August 7, 2012, https://www.timeout.com/chicago/things-to-do/what-its-like-to-work-for-rahm-emanuel (accessed July 19, 2017).

38. "Burge Pleads Innocent in Torture Case," *Chicago Tribune*, October 22, 2008.

39. Jason Meisner, "Lawyers Ask for Hearings on Prisoners Who May Be Victims of Jon Burge's Police Abuse," *Chicago Tribune*, October 17, 2008.

40. Aamer Madhani, "Chicago to Pay Reparations to Police Torture Victims," *USA Today*, April 14, 2015, https://www.usatoday.com/story/news/2015/04/14/chicago-to-pay-reparations-jon-burge-police-torture-victims/25766531/ (accessed May 27, 2017).

41. I was one of the reporters who went to Orlando, Florida, chasing Burge and trying to get a non-camera interview. I did get to speak with him over the phone, but he would not agree to go on camera with me.

42. *Wikipedia*, s.v. "Crime in Chicago," last edited June 6, 2017, https://en.wikipedia.org/wiki/Crime_in_Chicago.

43. Ibid.

44. Fredrick McKissack, "There's a Reason Black Youth Call Chicago 'Chiraq' and It's Not Just Criminals Doing the Shooting," *Huffington Post*, January 29, 2017, http://www.huffingtonpost.com/center-for-community-change-action/theres-a-reason-black-youth-call-chicago-chiraq_b_9110960.html (accessed July 19, 2017).

CHAPTER TWO: MURDER COVERAGE AS
A REFLECTION OF SOCIETY

1. After arriving at the scene a police spokesperson held a brief information update to let us know what they had found. Days later, authorities began to piece together the details and the names of the suspects were made public in local news outlets.

2. "Should Euthanasia or Physician-Assisted Suicide Be Legal?" ProCon.org, last updated March 9, 2017, http://euthanasia.procon.org/view.answers.php?questionID=001320 (accessed June 13, 2017).

3. Christy Gutowski, "Woman Convicted in Notorious Triple Murder: 'I Have Served Enough Time,'" *Chicago Tribune*, January 22, 2012.

4. Pat Curry, in interview with the author, August 15, 2013.

5. Kelly Barnicle, in interview with the author, August 20, 2013.

6. Curry, interview with the author.

7. Sandy Pudar, in interview with the author, August 5, 2013.

8. Ava Thompson Greenwell of the Medill School of Journalism, in interview with the author, March 14, 2014.

9. Marisa Rodriguez, in interview with the author, November 12, 2014.

10. Jennifer Lyons, in interview with the author, July 16, 2013.

11. Greg Caputo, in interview with the author, August 5, 2013.

12. Barnicle, interview with the author.

13. D. McQuail, *Mass Communication Theory: An Introduction* (London: Sage Publications, 1983).

14. P. M. Hirsch, with P. V. Miller and F. G. Kline, eds., *Occupational, Organizational, and Institutional Models in Mass Media Research: Toward an Integrated Framework* (Beverly Hills, CA: Sage Publications, 1997).

15. Reporters at one Chicago television station have told me

that they feared for their jobs if they did not come to daily meetings with their own story ideas. The pressure to increase ratings forced management to seek unusual techniques to improve the audience numbers.

16. Lyons, interview with the author.

17. Kevin Eck, "WDRB Explains Why It Thinks 'Breaking News' Is Broken," *TVSpy*, July 7, 2013, http://www.adweek.com/tvspy/wdrb-explains-why-it-thinks-breaking-news-is-broken/93749 (accessed September 20, 2013).

18. Dr. Carl C. Bell, in interview with the author, September 10, 2014. Carl C. Bell, MD, is a staff psychiatrist in the Psychosis Treatment Program and a professor in the Department of Psychiatry at the University of Illinois at Chicago College of Medicine. He is also a clinical professor of public health at the University of Illinois at Chicago School of Public Health. In addition, Dr. Bell is staff psychiatrist at Jackson Park Hospital's Family Medicine Center and St. Bernard Hospital's Inpatient Psychiatric Unit. He is the former director of the Institute of Juvenile Research and the former president/CEO of the Community Mental Health Council.

19. While I was working at CBS (1977–1980) each day I was required to make "beat checks." My office mate and I would split the United States down the middle—cities east or west of the Mississippi—and each of us would call every CBS affiliate assignment desk to determine what the big story of the day was. If there was a major event, we would report that to the bureau chief and a reporter could be sent to that city to cover the event.

20. B. W. Owen, *Economics and Freedom of Expression: Media Structure and the First Amendment* (Cambridge, MA: Ballinger, 1975).

21. D. Berkowitz and D. Beach, "News Sources and News Content: The Effect of Routine News, Conflict, and Proximity," *Journalism Quarterly* 6 (1993): 22.

22. Caputo, interview with the author.

23. Lyons, interview with the author.

24. Dwight DeWerth-Pallmeyer, *The Audience in the News* (Mahwah, NJ: Lawrence Erlbaum Associates, 1997).

25. Barnicle, interview with the author.

26. Phyllis Kaniss, *Making Local News* (University of Chicago Press, 1991).

27. Bell, interview with the author.

28. Ibid.

29. Ibid.

30. Pudar, interview with the author.

31. *Wikipedia*, s.v. "Gatekeeping (communication)," last edited May 7, 2017, https://en.wikipedia.org/wiki/Gatekeeping_(communication).

32. Curry, interview with the author.

33. This is a personal determination, as I only watch one TV station at a time and seldom if ever jump from one newscast to another. Likewise among my many friends, I know of one who switches back and forth during a newscast to see what is on the other stations.

34. Elyse Russo, in interview with the author, September 2013.

35. Chris Neale, in interview with the author, August 19, 2014.

36. Ibid. For more information about Dejero, visit their website at www.dejero.com.

37. "The Destination for Influential Explorers, the Destination for Influential Explorers," National Public Media, http://national publicmedia.com/pbs/audience/ (accessed July 22, 2017).

38. Over the years I have had numerous conversations with general managers and news directors who have repeated that the tag line "Chicago's very own" is a critically important marketing tool for drawing in viewers.

CHAPTER THREE: THE HISTORY OF THE
CHANGING BROADCAST FORMAT

1. Kendall, "138 Years of Murder in Chicago," Chicago Crime Scenes Project, July 21, 2009, http://chicagocrimescenes.blogspot .com/2009/07/138-years-of-murder-in-chicago.html (accessed May 2015).

2. "History of the Newsreel," http://sunnycv.com/steve/ filmnotes/newsreel.html (accessed July 22, 2017).

3. Aubrey Solomon, *The Fox Film Corporation, 1915–1935: A History and Filmography* (Austin: University of Texas Press, 2013).

4. "The March of Time," Old Time Radio, http://www.otr .com/march.html (accessed July 25, 2017).

5. Ibid.; *Wikipedia*, s.v. "The March of Time," last edited March 2, 2017, https://en.wikipedia.org/wiki/The_March_of_Time.

6. "Our History," Unshackled! https://unshackled.org/ about-us/our-history/ (accessed July 31, 2017).

7. "March of Time," Old Time Radio.

8. Dr. Carl C. Bell, in interview with the author, September 10, 2014.

9. The Cinema Products Company APS CP-16 R/A Operating Guide explains, "The Cinema Products CP-16 R/A is a portable 16 mm production camera noted for reliability and ease of use. Its integral shock mounting allows for silent/sync use without blimping, making it ideal for field interview work or studio application. It has the capability for single- as well as double-system sound use. Mic and line mixing can be done through the crystal sound electronics, which are part of the camera." "APS CP-16 R/A Operating Guide," Evergreen State College, last modified November 14, 2016, http://helpwiki.evergreen.edu/wiki/index .php/APS_CP-16_Operating_Guide (accessed June 13, 2017).

10. I understand that lighting person might be more politically

correct, but during this time there were no women working in television as members of the crews—not in lighting or sound or with cameras. That didn't begin until the 1980s and then slowly.

11. Greg Caputo, in interview with the author, August 5, 2013.

12. Ibid.

13. Robert Feder, "Pamela Jones Out as CBS 2 Reporter," *Robert Feder*, February 23, 2015, http://www.robertfeder.com/2015/02/23/pamela-jones-out-at-cbs-2/ (accessed July 22, 2017).

14. This was an in-house term used to describe the technicians and gear needed to go somewhere around the globe quickly.

15. Caputo, interview with the author.

16. Ibid.

17. Ibid.

18. Patricia Sullivan, "Frank N. Magid Dies at 78, Created News Anchor 'Happy Talk,'" *Washington Post*, February 8, 2010, http://www.washingtonpost.com/wp-dyn/content/article/2010/02/07/AR2010020702618.html (accessed July 22, 2017).

19. Consultants told news directors that news copy should be written in the present tense to give viewers a sense of immediacy.

20. Fr. Michael Louis Pfleger, in interview with the author, June 18, 2015.

21. Bell, interview with the author.

22. Marisa Rodriguez, in interview with the author, November 12, 2014.

23. Ibid.

CHAPTER FOUR: SURVEY—DECIDING WHICH MURDER STORIES TO COVER

1. "Station Index," Broadcasting Information Guide, 2017, http://www.stationindex.com/tv/tv-markets (accessed November 2016).

2. The following elements of the study, along with respondent comments, from Robert H. Jordan, "The Impact of Viewers on Television Producers' Perception of the Importance of Murder Victims," diss., 2000.

3. Ryan Marx, "Chicago Homicide Data since 1957," *Chicago Tribune*, March 2, 2016, http://www.chicagotribune.com/news/local/breaking/ct-chicago-homicides-data-since-1957-20160302-htmlstory.html (accessed July 22, 2017).

CHAPTER FIVE: GOOD GUYS VS. BAD GUYS

1. Both Arthur Schopenhauer and Sigmund Freud have used this situation to describe what they feel is the state of the individual in relation to others in society. The hedgehog's dilemma suggests that despite goodwill, human intimacy cannot occur without substantial mutual harm, and what results is cautious behavior and weak relationships. *Wikipedia*, s.v. "Hedgehog's Dilemma," last edited July 11, 2017, https://en.wikipedia.org/wiki/Hedgehog%27s_dilemma.

2. Dosey Meisels, "Personal Space and Self-Protection," *Journal of Personality and Social Psychology*, https://www.scribd.com/document/252476190/Dosey-Meisels-1969-Personal-Space-and-Self-protection (accessed July 22, 2017).

3. Jeff Wise, *Extreme Fear: The Science of Your Mind in Danger* (New York: St. Martin's, 2009).

4. *The Godfather: Part II*, directed by Francis Ford Coppola, Paramount Pictures, 1974.

5. Double Dutch is playing jump rope with two ropes moving in opposite directions and one person or more jumping simultaneously. This involves at least three people total—one or more jumping and two turning the ropes. While the jump roping is

going on, the two people turning the ropes often recite rhymes in rhythm.

6. John L. McKnight, "Redefining Community," Heartland Institute, https://www.heartland.org/_template-assets/documents/publications/4296.pdf (accessed July 22, 2017).

7. Andra C. Ghent, Ruben Hernandez-Murillo, and Michael T. Owyang, "Race Redlining, and Subprime Loan Pricing" (working paper 2011-033B, Federal Reserve Bank of St. Louis–Research Division, 2011).

8. Changingminds.org is the largest site in the world on all aspects of how to change what others think, believe, feel, and do.

9. Sandy Pudar, in interview with the author, August 5, 2013.

10. Fr. Michael Pfleger, in interview with the author, June 18, 2015.

11. Ibid.

12. Pat Curry, in interview with the author, August 15, 2013.

13. Dr. Carl Bell, in interview with the author, September 10, 2014.

CHAPTER SIX: BAD GUYS VS. BAD GUYS

1. Al Wysinger, in interview with the author, April 18, 2014.

2. Fr. Michael Pfleger, Facebook post, April 14, 2014, 8:44 a.m., https://www.facebook.com/pastorpfleger/posts/10202606 429816378.

3. Wysinger, interview with the author.

4. Superintendent Garry McCarthy press conference, April 21, 2014. McCarthy spoke after a graduation ceremony for new police officers at Navy Pier in Chicago.

5. Whet Moser, "Garry McCarthy's New Chicago Crime Strategy: Social Networks, 'Hot People,'" *Chicago Magazine*, October 1,

2012, http://www.chicagomag.com/Chicago-Magazine/The-312/
October-2012/Garry-McCarthys-New-Chicago-Crime-Strategy-Social
-Networks-Hot-People/ (accessed June 2016).

6. Ibid.

7. Dr. Carl C. Bell, interview with the author, September 10, 2014.

8. Ava Thompson Greenwell, in interview with the author, March 14, 2014.

9. Kristine Phillips, "Drugs Are Killing So Many People in Ohio That Cold-Storage Trailers Are Being Used as Morgues," *Washington Post*, March 16, 2017, https://www.washingtonpost.com/news/to-your-health/wp/2017/03/16/drugs-are-killing-so-many-in-this -county-that-cold-storage-trailers-are-being-used-as-morgues/?utm _term=.e1a4ba8046fb (accessed July 24, 2017).

10. Jeremy Gorner, "Few Answers as Chicago Hit with Worst Violence in Nearly 20 Years," *Chicago Tribune*, December 30, 2016, http://www.chicagotribune.com/news/local/breaking/ct-chicago -violence-2016-met-20161229-story.html (accessed January 20, 2017).

11. Police report that victims of crime in many neighborhoods refuse to tell officers who the criminals are for fear of retaliation or being known as a "rat" who runs to police. This culture often hampers police efforts to catch criminals.

12. Wysinger, interview with the author.

13. Ibid.

14. "Quinn Signs New Laws to Help Ex-Offenders Gain Employment," *Progress Illinois*, August 5, 2013.

15. Ibid.

16. In many of Father Michael Pfleger's sermons, he admonishes his congregation to make phone calls to police to report crime.

17. Fr. Michael Pfleger, Facebook post, April 8, 2014, 12:56 p.m., https://www.facebook.com/FrMichaelPfleger/posts/10152291404 499407?stream_ref=5.

18. Fr. Michael Pfleger, in an interview with the author, June 18, 2015.

19. Ibid.

20. David Heinzmann, "Suspect Bought AK-47 in Indiana," *Chicago Tribune*, March 16, 2006, http://articles.chicagotribune. com/2006-03-16/news/0603160196_1_gun-shop-americans-for-gun -safety-gun-control-group-americans (accessed July 24, 2017).

21. Ibid.

22. Siretha Woods, mother of ten-year-old Siretha White, in interview with the author, April 18, 2014.

23. McCarthy, press conference.

24. Sean Leidigh, in interview with the author, November 22, 2014.

25. A reference to the days when a pay phone, located on every corner, only required a dime to make a call. Today, not only does a phone call cost much more, but there are no pay phones; all have been removed by the phone companies.

26. Frank Main, "Girl Believed to Be Gang Assassin before She Was Gunned Down," *Chicago Sun-Times*, June 6, 2014.

CHAPTER SEVEN: THE PHANTOM AUDIENCE IN US ALL

1. Anna Roberts, in interview with the author, August 13, 2013.

2. Elyse Russo, in interview with the author, September 2013.

3. E. E. Dennis, *Reshaping the Media* (Newbury Park, CA: Sage Publications, 1989).

4. Pat Curry, in interview with the author, August 15, 2013.

5. Ibid.

6. Jennifer Lyons, in interview with the author, July 16, 2013.

7. Roberts, interview with the author.

8. Chris Neale, in interview with the author, November 2013.

9. Ibid.

10. Greg Caputo, in interview with the author, August 5, 2013.

11. Ibid.

12. Natalie Costa, in interview with the author, August 17, 2013.

13. Nancy Ryan and Rob Karwath, "Mother Visited Gary Girl Locked in Freezing House," *Chicago Tribune*, January 23, 1988.

14. Costa, interview with the author.

15. Lyons, interview with the author.

16. "Dejero: Simplifying the Remote Acquisition, Cloud Management, and Multi-Screen Distribution of Professional Live Video over IP," Dejero, 2017, https://www.dejero.com/ (accessed July 22, 2017). Located in Kitchener, Ontario, Canada, Dejero offers the most extensive and versatile range of bonded wireless uplink solutions for mobile newsgathering.

17. Andrew Stern, "Chicago Braces for Violence at NATO Summit," *Chicago Tribune*, May 15, 2012.

18. Ibid.

19. Roger Yu, *USA Today*, "Tribune Buys 19 TV Stations to Broaden Its Reach," *Pacific Daily News*, July 1, 2013, http://www.guampdn.com/story/money/business/2013/07/01/tribune-to-acquire-19-tv-stations-for-273b/2478769/ (accessed, March 2015).

20. Robert Channick, "Tribune Co. Publishing Spinoff May Include $325 Million Dividend," *Chicago Tribune*, February 19, 2014.

CHAPTER EIGHT: PERSPECTIVE AND TRUTH

1. Quote attributed to Fabian Linden.

2. Polly Mosendz, "Dylann Roof Confesses: Says He Wanted to Start 'Race War,'" *Newsweek*, June 19, 2015, http://www.newsweek.com/dylann-roof-confesses-church-shooting-says-he-wanted-start-race-war-344797 (accessed July 23, 2017).

3. Peter Nickeas, "Fourth of July Weekend Toll: 82 Shot, 14 of Them Fatally, in Chicago," *Chicago Tribune*, July 7, 2014, http://

www.chicagotribune.com/news/local/breaking/chi-fourth-of
-july-toll-82-shot-14-of-them-fatally-in-chicago-20140707-story.html
(accessed July 23, 2017).

4. In 2015, Roof created a website called the Last Rhodesian, a
reference to the white-ruled African country, which fought a bitter
civil war against black majority rule before it became Zimbabwe.
Roof wrote, "I chose Charleston because it is the most historic
city in my state, and at one time had the highest ratio of blacks to
Whites in the country. We have no skinheads, no real KKK, no one
doing anything but talking on the internet. Well someone has to
have the bravery to take it to the real world, and I guess that has to
be me." Brendan O'Connor, "Here Is What Appears to Be Dylann
Roof's Racist Manifesto," *Gawker*, June 20, 2015, http://gawker
.com/here-is-what-appears-to-be-dylann-roofs-racist-manifest
-1712767241 (accessed July 23, 2017).

5. Cindy Schreuder, "The 1995 Chicago Heat Wave," *Chicago
Tribune*, July 14, 2015, http://www.chicagotribune.com/news/
nationworld/politics/chi-chicagodays-1995heat-story-story.html
(accessed July 24, 2017).

6. Associated Press, "1995—The Summer That Chicago
Sizzled," *USA Today*, July 11, 2005.

7. Ibid.

8. Melita Marie Garza with Bonnie Miller Rubin, "Last Heat
Victims Buried with No One to Mourn Them," *Chicago Tribune*,
August 26, 1995.

9. Karen Grigsby Bates, "In the Aftermath of Charleston, Many
Whites Ask What They Can Do to Fight Racism," NPR, June 28,
2015, http://www.npr.org/2015/06/28/418355208/in-the
-aftermath-of-charleston-many-whites-ask-what-they-can-do-to-fight
-racism (accessed July 24, 2017).

10. Andrew Lord, "6 Companies Ban Confederate Flag Sales,"
Huffington Post, June 23, 2015, http://www.huffingtonpost.com/

2015/06/23/retailers-ban-confederate-flags_n_7648614.html (accessed July 23, 2017).

11. Ava Thompson Greenwell, in interview with the author, March 14, 2014.

12. *Harvard Business Review* staff, "What Business Are You In? Classic Advice from Theodore Levitt," *Harvard Business Review*, October 2006.

13. Aaron Smith, "US Smartphone Use in 2015," Pew Research Center, April 1, 2015.

14. Ibid.

15. Elyse Russo, in interview with the author, September 2013.

16. Clayton M. Christensen, Theodore Levitt et al., *HBR's 10 Must-Reads on Strategic Marketing* (Boston, MA: Harvard Business Review Press, 2013).

17. Michael A. Memoli, "Obama Embraces Race, Religion in Moving Address at Charleston Funeral," *Los Angeles Times,* June 26, 2015, http://www.latimes.com/nation/la-na-obama-charleston -funeral-20150626-story.html (accessed October 2016).

18. Barack Obama, "Remarks by the President in Eulogy for the Honorable Reverend Clementa Pinckney" (eulogy, Charleston, South Carolina, June 26, 2015), Office of the Press Secretary, https://obamawhitehouse.archives.gov/the-press-office/ 2015/06/26/remarks-president-eulogy-honorable-reverend -clementa-pinckney (accessed July 23, 2017).

CHAPTER NINE: REALIGNING THE PROCESS FOR COVERING MURDERS

1. Bill Kovach and Tom Rosenstiel, *Warp Speed: America in the Age of Mixed Media* (New York: Century Foundation, 1999), pp. 6–7.

2. Dr. Carl C. Bell, in interview with the author, September 10, 2014.

3. Ava Thompson Greenwell, in interview with the author, March 14, 2014.

4. Ibid.

5. Greg Caputo, in interview with the author, August 5, 2013.

6. Amy Mitchell, "State of the News Media 2014," Pew Research Journalism Project, March 28, 2014.

7. Robert Feder, "Robservations: Whoa! Univision Didn't Win 10 P.M. Ratings After All," *Robert Feder,* July 6, 2017, http://www .robertfeder.com/2017/07/06/robservations-whoa-univision-didnt -win-10-p-m-ratings/ (accessed July 27, 2017). Ratings are important because advertising rates for the next four months are determined by viewership numbers that are obtained by the Nielsen Company. Nielsen is a global information and measurement company and the leader in TV and Internet research. Nielsen measures what people across the United States are watching on TV. This viewing information is used to provide TV stations with ratings.

8. Greenwell, interview with the author.

9. Jack Fuller, *What Is Happening to News: The Information Explosion and the Crisis in Journalism* (Chicago: University of Chicago Press, 2013).

10. Michael Lansu, in interview with the author, May 15, 2015.

11. Joseph Goldstein and Nate Schweber, "Man's Death after Chokehold Raises Old Issue for the Police," *New York Times,* July 18, 2014, https://www.nytimes.com/2014/07/19/nyregion/staten -island-man-dies-after-he-is-put-in-chokehold-during-arrest.html (accessed July 24, 2017).

12. Massimo Calabresi, "Why a Medical Examiner Called Eric Garner's Death a 'Homicide,'" *Time,* December 4, 2014, http:// time.com/3618279/eric-garner-chokehold-crime-staten-island -daniel-pantaleo/ (accessed July 26, 2017).

13. Cliff Gilley, "Why Should I Comply When a Police Officer Says 'Get on the Ground! Do It Now!?'" Quora, September 6, 2013,

https://www.quora.com/Why-should-I-comply-when-a-police
-officer-says-Get-on-the-ground-Do-it-now (accessed July 26, 2013).

14. Greenwell, interview with author.

15. Chris Neale, in interview with the author, November 2013.

16. Steve Schmadeke, "No Bail for Reputed Gang Member
Charged with Killing Special Ed Teacher," *Chicago Tribune*, June 12,
2014, http://www.chicagotribune.com/news/local/breaking/
chi-suspect-questioned-in-killing-of-teacher-betty-howard-20140611
-story.html (accessed July 23, 2017).

17. Ibid.

18. Lansu, interview with the author.

19. Al Wysinger, in interview with the author, November 20,
2015.

20. Lansu, interview with the author.

21. Clifford Christians, Mark Fackler, Kim B. Rotzoll, and Kathy
Brittain McKee, *Media Ethics: Cases and Moral Reasoning*, 5th ed.
(Boston: Addison-Wesley Educational Publishers, 1998).

22. Natalie Costa, in interview with the author, August 17, 2013.

23. Lansu, interview with the author.

24. Ibid.

25. Wysinger, interview with the author.

26. While serving in the army I worked as a surgical assistant
in the operating room. I scrubbed on deliveries when the wives of
servicemen gave birth. When I returned to school, I also scrubbed
part-time in the operating rooms of several civilian hospitals.

27. Jennifer Lyons, in interview with the author, July 16, 2013.

28. Ibid.

29. The term *Tao* means "way," "path," or "principle" and can
also be found in Chinese philosophies and religions other than
Taoism.

30. Confucius, *The Great Learning* (MIT Internet Classics Archive,
2009), http://classics.mit.edu/Confucius/learning.html. These

are rewritten excerpts translated from the original text, which was written ca. 500 BC.

    31. Ibid.

INDEX

ABC (television network), 91,
148, 165
  ABC News, 90
AC Nielsen Company, 34, 39
"Action News" format, 98
African Americans
  African Americans
    responding to news cov-
    erage survey, 113, 117
  and assignment editors, 91,
  97
  Barack Obama on race relations, 188
  joining with whites
    after Roof killings in
    Charleston, 179–81
  media coverage, 82, 189
    after 1983 more efforts
      to cover news in "black
      community," 97
    black teens as innocent
      victims, 120, 151
    of cell phone snatchings
      by black teens, 45–46
    double standard on white/
      black murder coverage,
      176, 177

of Emmett Till death, 84
of Eric Garner death,
  196–97
of Jon Burge's treatment
  of suspects, 49
minimal minority coverage
  in news, 94
on Nashville television stations, 88
negative stereotypes,
  80–81, 84, 88–89
newsreels, 86
representation of in,
  80–81, 84, 88, 191–92
of Trayvon Martin's death,
  49
at WGN-TV, 90–91 (*see
also* Jordan, Robert H.,
Jr.; neighborhoods in
Chicago)
age
  as factor in news coverage,
  40, 57–58, 119–20, 123,
  124–25
  of survey respondents, 113
  See also children; elderly
Alighieri, Dante, 25

231

INDEX

Amos 'n' Andy (radio program), 81, 84

anchors, 38, 113
    Jordan as an anchor, 10, 89, 90, 186
    "news is what I say it is," 43, 71, 77
    presentation styles of, 76, 97–99, 160, 171
    and social media, 185–86

Angotti, Gino, 29

Anthony, Carmelo, 31

Ardrey, Robert, 141

Aron, Levi, 29

"assembly-line" production of news stories, 43, 74–75, 165

assignment editors, 38
    and African Americans, 91, 97
    moral and ethical considerations, 202–209
    and the placement and construction of news stories, 39, 62–63, 68–71, 105, 111–12, 144, 165
    choosing lead story, 162
    choosing which murder to cover, 26, 35–36, 45, 50–51, 57–58, 109, 194, 197
    difficulty of deciding, 125, 127, 198–99, 204, 204–205, 207, 208
    disagreements on how to cover a story, 163–64
    looking at a story being "doable," 169
    needing to agree a story worth covering, 43–44, 73–74, 163
    shaping the "meanings" of news stories, 40
    taking into account age of murder victim, 40, 57–58
    use of "sources," 19–20
    relationship to the audience, 68–69, 70–71, 157–59, 161, 166
    and staff shortages, 203–204
    stress of job, 74
    surveyed on news events and news coverage, 70–71, 107, 111–24
    way to change thinking of, 206
    See also newsroom gatekeepers

Associated Press, 43, 87, 88

audience, 39, 157–74
    audience imagery, 40, 42, 71, 76, 157–59
    citizen journalists, 196
    drill vs. hole epigram, 184
    importance to success of a news program, 183

232

Internet metrics showing who is watching and when, 64, 68, 70, 73, 157–58
journalists' efforts to explain news to, 54–55, 65
not leaving sections of audience out, 69, 205, 206
not taking sides, 67, 104
marketing the news to, 72–73
creative ways to reach, 184–87
factors to draw audience into the news, 68–73
journalists' perceptions, 40–41
recognizing different demographic watching patterns, 134–35
ways to attract bigger audiences, 98
need to trust news coverages, 190
public perceptions, 41
influence of audience on journalism and news coverage, 157, 158, 159–60, 162–64
of reality, 50
reporters and assignment editors not thinking about, 157–59

role of in choice of news stories, 12, 15, 38–40, 40, 135, 159–60, 161
meaning of viewing patterns, 173–74
staff diversity affecting audience, 193–94, 198
use of by editors and producers to meet organizational needs, 71
watching one station at a time, 71, 72, 110
Aunt Jemima (syrup), 84
Aurelius, Marcus, 174

"bad guys"
antisocial actions of, 141
"bad guys vs. bad guys," 141–56
gangs automatically considered "bad guys," 58, 141, 143 (see also gangs in Chicago)
"good guys vs. bad guys," 80, 127–39
ignoring/ostracizing rather than understanding, 147
maintaining a code of silence, 141–43
not receiving the attention or help they need, 151–54
treatment of after found guilty, 148–50

Bange, Jackie, 186

banks and "redlining," 132–34

Barnes, Gakirah, 155–56

Barnicle, Kelly, 58, 63, 68–69

Basie, Count, 86

Beach, Douglas W., 67

Beck, Andrew, 108

Bell, Carl, 66, 69–70, 89, 101, 138, 146–47, 192

Berkowitz, Dan, 67

Berkowitz, David ("Son of Sam"), 188

Beta and VHS videotape formats, 93–94

"Black Lives Matter," 20–21

"Blue Lives Matter," 20–21

body cams, 20

Boston Police Department, 145

Bozo's Circus (WGN-TV show), 89

Bratton, William, 145

"breaking news" stories, 32, 39–40, 55, 64, 95, 209

    murder stories falling in this category, 56–58, 164

    over use of phrase, 76, 176

    planned stories turning into, 170–73

    reader deciding which murder stories to cover (*see* survey of news gatekeepers on news events and news coverage)

    smartphones as source of breaking news, 185

    techniques for presenting, 100

    See also news coverage

Britt, Darlwin, 168

broadcast formats, history of changes in, 79–105

"broken windows" theory (cracking down on minor offenses), 145

Brown, Floyd, 90

Brown, Gloria, 90

Burge, Jon, 48–49

Caesarian section on murder victim. *See under* children

Caffey, Fedell, 53–54

cameras, 20, 29

    and cell phones, 102

        Dejero-type boxes, 74, 102–103, 171–72

    changes in size of, 85–86, 91

    use of digital formats, 99–101

    use of with satellite feeds, 95–96

    videotape and news coverage, 91–92

Capone, Al, 188

Caputo, Greg, 40–41, 43, 62, 67–68, 71, 92, 94, 96–97, 165–66, 193

Carlisle, Darlwin, 167–69

CBS (television network), 37, 91, 92, 148

    CBS Evening News with Walter Cronkite, 93

    CBS Morning News, 93

    Jordan hired by CBS Network News, 92–93

    Midwest Bureau, 92, 93

cell phones, 172–73, 185

    cell phone snatchings leading to murder, 45–46

    and citizen journalists, 196

    Dejero-type boxes, 74, 102–103, 171–72

Charleston, SC, killings in black church, 176

    aftermath, 179–81

    impact on journalists, 188

Chicago

    Great Chicago Fire of 1871, 177

    heat wave of 1995, deaths during, 177–79

    as murder capital of US, 51, 107

    murder statistics, 28, 34–35, 44, 110, 149

        amount of news coverage given, 50–51

        causing more reporting of murders, 46

    growth of between 1870 and 1920, 82

    as a segregated city, 36

    See also gangs in Chicago; minority demographics, growth in; neighborhoods in Chicago

Chicago (magazine), 145

Chicago Police Department, 44, 47–48

    Citizens Academy, 206

    and community relations, 149, 151

    Jon Burge case, 48–49

    seen as "good guys," 143 (*see also* "good guys")

Chicago Sun-Times (newspaper), 45, 142, 143, 155, 195

"Chicago's Very Own" (tagline for WGN-TV), 76

Chicago Tribune (newspaper), 28, 35, 57, 101, 195, 199, 204

children, 121, 135, 160

    Caesarian section on murder victim, 53–55

    child in a freezing attic, 167–69

    and drugs, 148

        impact of mother's drug use on, 146–47, 168

    killing of innocent children, 53, 153, 154, 163–64,

207 (*see also* Pendleton, Hadiya; White, Siretha)
need to protect, 127–28
receiving more news coverage, 119–20, 124
coverage given to school kids vs. gang members, 120–22
Chinese Americans, media coverage during radio years, 82
Christians, Clifford, 202–203
cinema. *See* Fox Movietone newsreels
citizen journalists, 196
Citizens Academy, 206
Clinton, Hillary, 19
CLTV, 27, 163, 199
CLTV.com, 157
CNN (television network), 34, 95, 102, 191
code of silence, 141–43, 149
ComEd (electricity supplier), 178
Common, Devin, 29
computerized crime fighting, 144–46
CompStat System, 145–46
Confederate flag and response to Charleston killings, 180
conflict as a criteria for covering a story, 56, 77, 208
Confucius, applying to modern journalism, 208–209

consequences (element of news), 176, 208
unintended consequences, 179–81
Corleone, Vito (fictional character), 130–31
Costa, Natalie, 166, 169, 203–204
craft and entrepreneurship, 75
Crawford, Jack, 168
cultural changes in US affecting news coverages, 79–105, 190
impact on Jordan, 80–81, 82–84, 85–86, 87–93
newsreels, 84–86
radio years, 80–82, 84
and smartphones and apps, 102–104
and social media, 101–105
television years, 88, 90–101
growth of importance of news coverage, 96–101
Current Affair (TV program), 96
Curry, Pat, 35–36, 57, 58, 70, 137, 159, 161

Dahmer, Jeffrey, 188
Daley, Richard, 178
Dante. *See* Alighieri, Dante
dashboard cameras, 20
Davis, Sammy, Jr., 86
Dee, Merri, 90

Dejero-type boxes, 102, 103, 171–73

demonizing others, 134–39

Dennis, Everette, 158

Dennis, Medrid, 83–84

"Developing Story." *See* "breaking news" stories

digital formats and news coverage, 99–101, 102

distrust of police, 142–43, 149

diversity, need for in newsrooms, 193–94, 205

drill vs. hole epigram, 184

drive-by murders and the "wow" effect, 68–69

Drudge Report (online news), 165

drugs and drug traffic, 53, 137
  and gangs, 25, 134, 150, 155, 202
  heroin addiction, 147–48
  impact of on mothers and children, 146–47, 168
  in upscale and inner-city neighborhoods, 144–45
  War on Drugs, 148

economics, news dependent on "assembly-line" production of news stories, 43, 74–75, 165
  news as a "loss leader" in the 1980s, 96

news becoming economically important to stations, 97–98

news directors' responsibilities, 67–68, 71, 72, 75, 97, 98

See also marketing the news; socioeconomic level

editors, 10, 12, 21
  and expansion of Internet news, 101–102
  and "sensational" or "breaking" stories, 30–31, 39, 51, 72, 159
  thinking about the audience, 40, 41, 46, 70, 71, 77, 158–59
  See also assignment editors; newsroom gatekeepers

elderly, 100, 119, 120, 151, 177–78, 179

election coverage, 19, 97, 170–73

electronic newsgathering (ENG) work, 95–96. *See also* satellites and media coverage

Elements of Journalism, The: What Newspeople Should Know and the Public Should Expect (Kovach and Rosenstiel), 44, 207–208

Ellington, Duke, 86

Emanuel, Rahm, 34, 48, 205

Emanuel African Methodist Episcopal Church, killings at, 175–77

eminence. *See* prominence of people involved in a news story

ENG. *See* electronic newsgathering (ENG) work

ethics. *See* moral and ethical duties of journalists

ethnicity, 36, 117, 130–32
    of murder victim as factor on news coverage, 111, 116–17, 120, 124, 143–44
    and "redlining," 132–34
    See also African Americans; Hispanics; minority demographics, growth in

Evans, Deborah, 53–55, 56–57, 65, 77

exclusive news coverage, 9, 110

ex-offenders, 149–50

Extreme Fear: The Science of Your Mind in Danger (Wise), 129

Facebook, 21, 35, 42, 101, 102, 103, 104, 143–44, 151, 186, 195

Fackler, Mark, 202–203

families and neighbors. *See* neighborhoods in Chicago

Farr, Christian, 90

Farr, Karen (Jordan), 90

Feder, Robert, 194

females in the newsroom. *See under* gender

Final Cut Pro (news editing program), 100

Fisk University, 87, 88

Fitzgerald, Ella, 86

Fortune (magazine), 37

Fox Movietone newsreels, 84–85, 86

Fuller, Jack, 195

gangs in Chicago, 21–22
    automatically seen as "bad guys," 58, 141, 143
    Gakirah Barnes as a female gang assassin, 155–56
    "good guys vs. bad guys," 127–30, 131–32
    and illegal drugs, 25, 134, 150, 155, 202
    negative perceptions about, 70, 135–36, 150–51
        leading to less news coverage, 141
    newsroom gatekeepers choosing coverage of, 117–18, 194
        ranking of death of Hispanic gang member vs. other Hispanics, 123

school kids vs. gang members, 120–22

police fight against computerized crime fighting, 145, 146

needing more presence in high-crime neighborhoods, 201–202

social structure, 130

binding members together, 127–28

dislike of intense media coverage of selves, 154–55

giving up a member if crime is getting enough attention, 155

need for "street cred," 146

reasons for joining, 152

WGN-TV policy on reporting gang murders, 27, 57

See also "bad guys"

Garner, Eric, 196–97

Gary, IN, 94

and child freezing in attic, 167–69

"Gatekeeper" study by White, 70–71

gender

females in the newsroom, 90, 113, 193

and treatment in the news,

39–40, 40, 50, 58, 110–11, 122–23, 177, 183

Ghent, Andra C., 133

Godfather, The: Part II (movie), 130

"good guys"

Chicago Police seen as, 143

"good guys vs. bad guys," 127–39

Google Analytics (website traffic reporting service), 64, 73

Granich, Jeff, 30

great apes, social network of, 129–30

Great Chicago Fire of 1871. *See under* Chicago

Green, Al, 87, 88

Greenwell, Ava Thompson, 59–60, 147–48, 182–83, 192–93, 194, 198, 205

gut instinct on newsworthiness, 26, 42, 60, 70, 73–78, 122, 161, 162–63, 166, 169, 208

"hard" news

importance of timeliness and use of inverted pyramid style of writing story, 65

vs. "softer" news, 46–47, 64

Harrison, Chuck, 89–90

Harvard Business Review (magazine), 184–85, 187

Harvard Business School, 184

headlines, 41, 152

"headline magic," looking for in choosing stories, 60–61 (*see also* "sensational" status of some news stories)

impact of, 46–48

use of to create interest in a story, 10, 32, 40, 45, 171, 199

overuse of, 64, 76

and videos, 197

"hedgehog's dilemma," 128–29

helicopters, use of to cover news stories, 50, 62, 67, 75, 89

Hernandez-Murillo, Ruben, 133

high-crime neighborhoods. *See* neighborhoods in Chicago

high-profile cases. *See* "sensational" status of some news stories

Hines, Burleigh, 91

Hirsch, Paul M., 63

Hispanics, 31, 123, 133, 143, 183, 191–92, 193

change in viewer demographic, 193–94

ranking of death of Hispanic gang member vs. other Hispanics for news coverage, 123

"hoodies" and the Trayvon Martin murder, 31

Horne, Lena, 86

Houston, TX, 33

Howard, Betty, 199–200

human interest stories, 37, 46, 64

as a criteria for covering a story, 77

See also "softer" news

image and imagery. *See* audience: audience imagery; product image of news stories

immediacy (element of news), 65, 98, 174, 208

immigrants, 82, 119, 120, 130, 131–32, 193

inner-city neighborhoods. *See* neighborhoods in Chicago

Innocence Project, 141

Inside Edition (TV program), 96

Instagram, 104

Internet news

choosing stories with "headline magic," 60–61

ethical issues for, 158

importance of comments section, 60, 163, 190

importance to success of a news program, 68, 102, 183

as way to attract viewers to televised news, 186
web analytics, 41–42
and Google Analytics, 64
inverted pyramid style of writing, 65
iPads, 104
Isaac, Richard "Ike," 90, 167, 168

Jet (magazine), 84
Jordan, Karen. *See* Farr, Karen
Jordan, Robert H., Jr., 80–81, 82–84, 85–86, 87–93, 189
 on covering death of Deborah Evans, 53–55
 on covering scandal rather than murders, 9–13
 on covering story of child freezing in attic, 167–69
Jordan, Sharon, 90
journalism and journalists, 19, 22–23, 42, 60, 70, 73–78, 122, 161–63, 166, 169, 208
 applying Confucius and Taoism to, 207–209
 changes in, 19, 79–105, 190, 196 (*see also* Internet news; social media platforms)
 elements of the news, 65, 77, 190–91
 ethical and moral con-
siderations, 13, 158, 202–209
 influence of audience on, 157, 158, 159–60, 162–63, 164
 intuitive judgment, 26
 and objectivity, 13, 21, 56, 67, 198
 obligations and principles of, 44–45, 67, 190
 teaching of journalism, 147–48, 192, 194, 198
 what is and isn't news, 42–46
 See also assignment editors; newsroom gatekeepers; reporters; survey of news gatekeepers on news events and news coverage

Kaniss, Phyllis, 69
Kellogg School of Management (Northwestern University), 63
Kennedy, John F., 85
King, Martin Luther, Jr., 189
King, Rodney, 20, 196, 197
Kletzky, Leiby, 28–29
Kovach, Bill, 44, 190–91, 207–208

Lansu, Michael, 195, 200–202, 204–205
Larsen, Roy, 86

Latinos. *See* Hispanics

Leidigh, Sean, 154

Levin, Jennifer, 28

Levitt, Theodore, 184

LHT Consulting Group, 33

Lindbergh, Charles, 85

Linden, Fabian, 175

Liston, Sonny, 127

"live shots," 54, 96, 101, 115, 165

Local TV Holdings (broad-
casting company), 173

location of murder as factor
on news coverage, 110–11,
118–19, 120, 123, 124, 144
reporters sometimes going
into an area blind, 161

Los Angeles, CA, 29, 51. *See also*
King, Rodney; Simpson, O. J.

Loyola University, 108

Luce, Henry, 43

Lyons, Jennifer, 27, 41–42, 47,
60–61, 64, 68, 162, 170, 207

Magid, Frank, 98

Making Local News (Kaniss), 69

Manson, Charles, 188

March of Time (radio program), 86

marketing the news, 40–42, 64,
76, 82

Martin, Trayvon, 31–32

*Mass Communications Theory: An
Introduction* (McQuail), 63

McCarthy, Garry, 30, 34, 145–46,
153–54

McEwen, Arthur, 42

McKee, Kathy, 202–203

McKnight, John, 132

McQuail, Denis, 63

media coverage. *See* news
coverage

*Media Ethics: Cases and Moral
Reasoning* (Christians, Fackler,
Rotzoll, and McKee), 202–203

Medill School of Journalism,
147–48, 192, 194, 198

Meharry Medical College, 88

Miami Heat (basketball team), 31

minority demographics, growth
in, 25–26, 193
need for diversity in newsrooms, 205
See also African Americans;
ethnicity; Hispanics; Native
Americans; race

Mitchell, Brian, 188

mobile devices. *See* cell phones;
iPads

Mona Lisa, destruction of, 77

Moonves, Leslie, 37

moral and ethical duties of journalists, 13, 158, 202–209

Morehouse College, 87

mourning of prominent murder
victims, 32–34

Movietone newsreels. *See* Fox Movietone newsreels

National Weather Service, 88
Native Americans, 81, 146–47
NATO summit in Chicago (2012), 102, 172–73
NBC (television network), 87, 90–91, 165
Neale, Chris, 74, 163–64, 198–99
neighborhoods in Chicago, 25–26, 88, 131, 142–43, 149, 165, 205
 affluent neighborhoods, 123, 144–45
 high-crime neighborhoods, 123, 144, 147, 200, 201
 importance of families and neighborhoods in determining news coverage of a murder, 59–60
 inner-city neighborhoods, 22, 69, 100, 114, 123, 131–32, 133, 134, 144–45, 147, 150–51
 minority neighborhoods, 57, 88, 91, 94, 133, 148, 191, 194 (*see also* minority demographics, growth in)
 use of neighborhood names as code for race of residents, 36, 136

news coverage
 "assembly-line" production of news stories, 43, 74–75, 165
 categories and types of news stories, 64–68 (*see also* "breaking news" stories; "hard" news; planned stories; "softer" news)
 change in content of news coverages, 191–92
 criteria for covering, 56, 77–78, 208
 choosing to cover a single death over casualties in another country, 50
 determining time for and order of news stories, 160–61
 determining what is news and what isn't, 73–78
 criteria for, 77–78
 difficulty of deciding, 207
 news gatekeepers filtering out for news coverage, 138
 See also survey of news gatekeepers on news events and news coverage
 "doable" news stories, 169–70
 elements of the news, 208

gangs disliking intense media coverage of selves, 154–55

gut instinct on newsworthiness, 42, 60, 70, 73–78, 122, 161, 162–63, 166, 169, 208

impact of staff shortages on coverage, 204

impact of too many murder stories, 195–96

importance of choosing story subjects, 198–200

moral duties of journalists, 202–203

ethical and moral considerations when judging murder stories, 203–209

murder cases

chosen for coverage, 65–66, 152, 187

criteria for newsworthiness, 77–78

examples of decisions on which murders receive coverage, 110–11

as "hard" news, 64–65

history of changing broadcast formats for covering, 79–105

importance given to some victims but not others, 109

involving prominent individuals, 72–73

reader becoming a gatekeeper deciding which murder stories to cover (*see* survey of news gatekeepers on news events and news coverage)

nature of is to look for the unusual events, 182

new mixed-media culture, 190–91

people involved in (*see* assignment editors; editors; journalism and journalists; newsroom gatekeepers; producers; reporters)

pressures on, 190

product image of news stories, 75–77 (*see also* audience: audience imagery)

role of audience (*see* audience: role of in choice of news stories)

standard routines and cycles in newsgathering process, 63

use of different mediums to view, 185–87

See also audience; "breaking news" stories; headlines;

"sensational" status of some news stories

news directors, 62, 75, 148, 162, 186, 187
    and economics of news coverage, 67–68, 71, 72, 75, 97, 98
    overseeing the entire news story, 75
    seeing importance of Internet news, 186
"news is what I say it is" model, 43, 71, 77
newspaper industry, shrinking of, 173, 184
newsreels as news coverage. *See* Fox Movietone newsreels
newsroom gatekeepers, 12, 19–20, 107, 127, 175, 190–91
    filtering news, 19, 35–36, 75, 108–109, 111, 112, 138, 141
    "Gatekeeper" study by White, 70–71
    and Jon Burge case, 49
    minorities as, 91
    moral and ethical duties of journalists, 13, 158, 203–209
    See also assignment editors; news directors; producers; survey of news gatekeepers

on news events and news coverage

New York City, murders in, 28–29, 51, 82, 196–97
New York Police Department, 145
New York Times (newspaper), 101
Nielsen ratings. *See* AC Nielsen Company

Obama, Barack, 188
Obama, Michelle, 28
objectivity, 13, 21, 56, 67, 198
oddity (element of news), 208
"Og, the Fire Keeper," 33, 80, 105
O'Keefe, Pat, 178
Ong, Ta, 108
"original reporting," 63
"others," creation of mentality of viewing ourselves and others, 23, 134–39, 146, 192, 202
Owen, Bruce M., 67
Owyang, Michael T., 133

Pacific Garden Mission (Chicago), 86
Pendleton, Hadiya, 28, 29–30, 46, 59–60, 152, 194
Periscope (app), 103
personal space, 129
Petty, Bob, 91

Pew Research, 185
    Pew Research Journalism
        Project, 193
Pfleger, Michael, 100, 135,
    136–37, 143–44, 150, 151–52,
    207
pilot study. *See* survey of news
    gatekeepers on news events
    and news coverage
Pinckney, Clementa (eulogy
    for), 188
planned stories, 56, 59, 169–70
    turning into breaking news,
        170–73
police methods of fighting
    crime
        "broken windows" theory
            (cracking down on minor
            offenses), 145
        computerized crime
            fighting, 144–46
        new programs, 154
police misconduct, 20, 21, 49,
    149
        Eric Garner case, 196–97
        Jon Burge case, 48–49
        Rodney King video, 20, 196
"porcupine's dilemma," 128–29
pornography and the VHS for-
    mat's popularity, 94
Porterfield, Harry, 91
"Preppie Murder Case," 28

preventable murders, 30
producers, 9, 10, 19–20, 38, 40,
    71–72, 91, 97, 100, 125, 127,
    148, 165, 206
    and audience, 12, 37–38, 40,
        41, 70–71, 77, 134–35, 157,
        161
    on "backstage" adjustments,
        59
    and coverage of murders, 26,
        27, 35, 39–40, 70, 96, 208
    editorial meetings, 33, 159,
        171
    exhaustion of, 127, 144
    fearing news becoming
        "stale," 72
    filling news slots, 169, 171
        slow days, 62–63
    moral and ethical duties of,
        202–209
    overseeing the entire news
        story, 75
    role of, 38, 39, 59, 68, 75–76,
        159
        deciding on newsworthi-
            ness, 43–44, 77–78
        filtering news, 169, 171
    use of neighborhood names
        rather than mentioning
        ethnic groups, 36, 136
    using same feedback as
        Internet news, 68

See also Internet news; news-room gatekeepers; survey of news gatekeepers on news events and news coverage; web producers

product image of news stories, 42, 75–76, 158

values found in, 76–77

See also audience: audience imagery

prominence of people involved in a news story, 199, 208

as a criteria for covering a story, 77

as a factor determining news coverage, 110–11, 123, 124

of victims, 39

proximity (relevance to local viewers), 77, 208

publishing, slowdown in, 173, 184

Pudar, Sandy, 26–27, 59, 70, 135

Pulitzer, Joseph, 195

Quall, Ward, 90

questionnaire used in survey of news events and news coverage, 111–24

race, 125, 192

of murder suspect as factor on news coverage, 123–24

of murder victim as factor on news coverage, 111, 116–17, 122, 123–24, 143–44

need for integrated staff in newsrooms, 91, 193

and "redlining," 132–34

See also minority demographics, growth in

"Race, Redlining, and Subprime Loan Pricing" (Federal Reserve study), 133

radio and news coverage, 80–82, 84, 86–87

differences between radio and television, 87

Ramsey, JonBenet, 50

ratings, 36–37, 96, 97, 110, 111–12, 163, 194

definition of, 38–39

use of in-depth stories or specials during ratings months, 154, 170

recidivism, reducing, 149–50

"redlining," 132–34

reporters, 38

and audience, 71, 157–59

changes in reporting, 19, 61–62

changing broadcast formats, 79–105

use of smartphones at scene, 185

interaction with other newsroom staff, 19, 38, 51,
63, 73, 159, 171 (*see also*
survey of news gatekeepers
on news events and news
coverage)
coordination of stories as
craft, 75
job requirements, 23,
182–83, 192, 198, 203, 208
accuracy, 55
journalistic elements,
65–68
moral and ethical duties
of, 202–209
need for more in-depth
coverage, 154, 160
search for truth, 44, 165,
175, 184, 208–209
time needed, 199
understanding newswor-
thiness, 43–44, 73–74
and murder coverage, 56–63,
147, 155, 160–61, 165, 174
choosing which murder to
cover when there is only
one reporter, 45, 114–17,
118–19
Dylann Roof murder case,
175–77, 179–81, 188
needing to dig deeper,
30–31, 35

using successful stories as
basis for covering others,
75–76
political reporting, 170–71
Reshaping the Media (Dennis),
158
Reynolds, Mel, 9–12
sexual assault case and, 9–12
Roberts, Anna, 157, 163, 183
Rodriguez, Marisa, 60, 102, 104
Roof, Dylann Storm, 175–77,
179–81, 188
Rosenblum, Mort, 43
Rosenstiel, Tom, 44, 190–91,
207–208
Rosten, Leo, 42
Rotzoll, Kim, 202–203
routines helping news organizations deal with gathering news,
63, 66–67, 71, 125, 164–65
Russo, Elyse, 37, 73, 158, 186

Sanford, FL (Trayvon Martin
murder), 31–32
Sanity of Survival, The (Bell), 66
satellites and media coverage,
94–95, 103
electronic newsgathering
(ENG) work, 95–96
Schopenhauer, Arthur, 128–29
"sensational" status of some
news stories, 12, 46–48

causing more public attention of police department and city officials, 47–48, 155

coverage of to raise TV ratings, 36–38

examples of high-profile cases, 26–32

factors that make a case "sensational," 30–31

impact of headline stories, 46–48

mourning of prominent murder victims, 32–34

potentially alerting audience to dangers, 46

Pulitzer advocating, 195

reasons Pendleton considered as, 60, 152

See also headlines; news coverage

"Sergeant Preston of the Yukon" (radio program), 80–81, 82

"sidebar" associated stories, 109

Simpson, Carole, 91

Simpson, O. J., 29, 72, 111, 188

60 Minutes (TV show), 148

smartphones. *See* cell phones

Smith, Jack, 92

Smith, Susan, 188

Snapchat, 104

snitch, not being a, 141–43, 149

Snyder, Vanessa, 29

social media platforms, 195

and changes in news coverage, 101–105

and presidential election of 2016, 19

See also Facebook; Instagram; Snapchat; Twitter

socioeconomic level, 70, 80, 192

personal perceptions of news staff, 122

of victim and impact of on news coverage, 40, 123, 124, 132

"softer" news, 37

timeliness and inverted pyramid style of writing less important to, 65

vs. "hard" news, 46–47, 64

See also human interest stories

statistics on responses to survey on news coverage, 113–14

question 18 (suspect or victim more interesting to viewers), 122

question 19 (race of the victim affecting decision), 122

questions 32 and 33 (race of victim and race of suspect), 123–24 scenario #1 (two murders only one reporter available), 116

scenario #2 (two murders in very different locations), 117

scenario #3 (choosing which gang murder to cover), 118

scenario #4 (location of murder determining coverage), 119

scenario #5 (age of victim determining coverage), 120

scenario #7 (location of murder determining coverage), 120

scenario #8 (murder of school kids vs. gang members), 121

statisticians consulting on survey concerning news coverage of murder cases, 108

stereotypes, 134, 138–39

Super Bowl as high-rating program, 36–37

surveillance cameras, 29

survey of news gatekeepers on news events and news coverage, 108–112

question 18 (suspect or victim more interesting to viewers), 122

scenario #1 (two murders only one reporter available), 114–16

scenario #2 (two murders in very different locations), 116–17

scenario #3 (choosing which gang murder to cover), 117–18

scenario #4 (location of murder determining coverage), 118–19

scenario #5 (age of victim determining coverage), 119–20

scenario #7 (location of murder determining coverage), 120

scenario #8 (murder of school kids vs. gang members), 120–22

suspects

need for people to report suspects to police, 200–201

treatment of by Burge, 48–49

victim or suspect most interesting to viewers, 46, 48, 122, 199–200

suspense (element of news), 208

tabloid news coverage, 28, 96–97

Tao ("the Way") applying concepts to journalism, 208

television and news coverage, 83–84, 88, 90–101, 190

  adopting "Action News" format, 98

  growth of, 96–101, 173

  seeing shrinking market shares, 186–87

  and smartphones and apps, 102–104

  and social media, 101–105

  use of Dejero-type boxes, 102, 103, 171–73

  use of digital formats, 99–101, 102

  use of satellites, 94–95, 103

  use of videotaping, 91–92, 93–94, 99

Tennessee State University, 88

Till, Emmett Louis, 84

Tilmon, Jim, 91

Time Inc. (company), 86

timeliness, importance of in "hard" news stories, 65

top story, 38, 44, 75, 110, 170, 197

  definition of, 39

Tribune Company Broadcasting, 173. *See also Chicago Tribune*; WGN-TV

Trump, Donald, 19

  criticisms of media, 23

trust

  news departments need from audience, 190

  police need to build, 149, 201

truth

  perspective and truth, 175–88

  reporter's search for truth, 44, 165, 175, 184, 208–209

Turner, Ted, 191

20/20 (TV show), 148

Twitter, 19, 21, 35, 101, 102, 104, 143, 151, 195

  people getting news from, 41–42, 165, 166

  use of in newsroom, 185–86

Univision, 194

Unshackled (radio program), 86–87

US Census Bureau, 36

US Federal Reserve, 133

"us" vs. "them," creation of mentality of, 23, 134–39, 146, 192, 202

VHS and Beta videotape formats, 93–94

victims, 40

mourning of prominent
murder victims, 193–94

newsroom gatekeepers fil-
tering out some for news
coverage, 19, 35–36, 108–
109, 111, 112, 138, 141

prominence of and news
coverage, 32–34, 39

relatives wondering why
there was no coverage of
murder of, 156

victim or suspect most interesting to viewers, 122, 123,
161

videos, videotape, and news coverage, 91–92, 99

impact of Eric Garner video,
196–97

Rodney King video, 20–21

impact of, 20, 196–97

use of cell phones to create,
21

VHS and Beta formats,
93–94

violence

causes of, 147

levels of, 35, 70, 101, 142,
144

Wall Street Journal (newspaper),
101

Wally Phillips radio show, 89

Ward, Laverne, 53–54

Ward, Michael, 29–30

Washington, Harold, 97

Washington Post (newspaper),
101

WBBM-TV, 92, 94, 193

web analytics, 41–42

and Google Analytics, 64

web producers, 37, 73, 102, 186

choosing stories with "headline magic," 60–61

paying attention to audience
metrics, 157–58, 183

and value of comment
section, 163

See also Internet news;
producers

Western Corral (television
program), 83, 87

WGBO (Chicago Spanish language station), 194

WGN-TV, 27, 173

becoming a superstation, 93,
95

changing amount of time
spent covering news, 191

decision making on what
stories are covered, 27,
35–39

Jordan's tenure at, 89–92, 93

pilot study on news events
and news coverage (*see*

survey of news gatekeepers on news events and news coverage)

policy on reporting gang murders, 27, 57

WGN-TV.com, 157

What Is Happening to News: The Information Explosion and the Crisis in Journalism (Fuller), 195

White, David M., 70

White, Siretha, 153

Williams, Jacqueline, 53–54, 56–57

Williams, Kenneth, 29–30

Winfrey, Oprah, 88

Wise, Jeff, 129

Woods, Siretha, 153

WSM Television, 87–88, 89

Wu, Linlin, 108

Wysinger, Al, 47, 142, 144, 149, 201, 206

Yale University, 35

Zimmerman, George, 31–32